Contents

INTERNATIONAL DICTIONARY OF
Accounting Acronyms

2ND EDITION

JAE K SHIM, MBA, PHD

Professor of Business
California State University, Long Beach
and
CEO
Delta Consulting Company

GLOBAL
professional
publishing

Global Professional Publishing Limited

Random Acres.

Slip Mill lane

Hawkhurst

TN18 5AD

England

ISBN: 978-1-906403-35-5

Printed and bound in Great Britain by 4Edge

For full details of Global Professional Publishing titles in
Accounting, Management, Finance and Banking
see our website at www.gppbooks.com

Preface

The *International Dictionary of Accounting Acronyms 2nd edition* contains approximately 2,000 accounting and related acronyms in current usage from a variety of areas of practice both in the USA, UK and many other countries. Subject areas coversvirtually all functional areas of business – accounting, taxes, business and management, business law, HRM, banking, finance, economics, investments, real estate, information technology (IT), management science, and statistics.

This volume is not intended to be either authoritative or exhaustive. Nor does the inclusion of an acronym represent an expression of the publisher's opinion as to any trademark or other rights in an acronym. The *Dictionary* should not be relied upon as having any bearing upon the validity or ownership of any trademark. The failure to indicate that an acronym is a trademark is not intended to represent that no trademark exists in the acronym and does not affect any legal rights in such acronym. A reference to an owner of an acronym or to an acronym as a trademark likewise should not be relied upon for legal authority. Errors brought to the attention of the publisher and verified satisfactorily will be corrected in future editions.

Effort has been made to exclude terms that are obsolete or of extremely limited current use, and terms of only local interest. Acronyms and their terms that are seldom or no longer used, but have been superseded by other terminology, are included because some discussions and documents may involve the older terminology, if only because those terms made strong impressions during their long years of use.

Acronyms concerning business and professional services relevant to the practice of accounting are included to anticipate terms that a user may encounter in range of situations where an individual may be expected to be familiar with the vernacular.

Acronyms with multiple meanings, all of them in current usage, will be listed in alphabetical order of their spelled-out meaning. However, most acronyms still require a brief explanation of their meaning in addition to a spelled-out meaning. Therefore, a supplemental explanation has been given to aid the user in understanding the acronym and the term it represents. Otherwise, it is generally expected that the user will be able to again rely on the context of the discussion or relevant documents to guide him or her to the correct terminology.

About the Author

Dr. Jae K. Shim is one of the most prolific accounting and finance experts in the world. He is a professor of business at California State University, Long Beach and CEO of Delta Consulting Company, a financial consulting and training firm. Dr. Shim received his M.B.A. and Ph.D. degrees from the University of California at Berkeley (Haas School of Business). Dr. Shim has been a consultant to commercial and nonprofit organizations for over 30 years.

Dr. Shim has over 50 college and professional books to his credit. Thirty of his publications have been translated into foreign languages such as Chinese, Spanish, Russian, Polish, Croatian, Italian, Japanese, and Korean. Professor Shim's books have been published by CCH, Barron's, John Wiley, McGraw-Hill, Prentice-Hall, Penguins Portfolio, Thomson Reuters, Global Publishing, American Management Association (Amacom), and the American Institute of CPAs (AICPA).

Dr. Shim has also published numerous articles in professional and academic journals. He was the recipient of the Financial Management Association International's *1982 Credit Research Foundation Award* for his article on cash flow forecasting and financial modeling.

Dr. Shim has been frequently quoted by such media as the *Los Angeles Times, Orange County Register, Business Start-ups, Personal Finance, and Money Radio*. He also provides business content He also provides business content for CPE e-learning providers and for m-learning providers such as iPhone, iPad, iPod, Blackberry, Android, Droid, and Nokia.

Accounting
Acronyms

A

AAA **Accumulated Adjustment Account**

Under Section 1368(e)(1) of the IRS Code, an account of the S corporation which is adjusted for the S period in a manner similar to the adjustments under 1367 (except that no adjustment shall be made for income (and related expenses) which is exempt from tax under title 26 and the phrase '(but not below)' shall be disregarded in 1367(b)(2)(A)) and no adjustment shall be made for Federal taxes attributable to any taxable year for a C corporation.

American Accounting Association
(aaahq.org)

Organization primarily of accounting academicians emphasizing the development of a theoretical foundation for accounting. Its research with respect to education and theory is distributed through committee report and a quarterly journal, *The Accounting Review*.

AAII **American Association of Individual Investors**
(www.aaii.com)

Based in Chicago, an independent, nonprofit corporation formed in 1978 for the purpose of assisting individuals in becoming effective managers of their own assets through programs of education, information, and research. Its flagship publication is AAII Journal.

AAPC **Adjusted Average Per Capita Cost**

Business accounting and marketing term relating to adjustments made to average per capita costs to increase the accuracy of an analysis.

AAR **Against All Risks**

Insurance term (applied elsewhere as well) to identify condition of having identified risks connected with a planned insured or other venture.

AARS **Accrual Accounting and Reporting System**

Accounting term describing treatment of revenues when expected

to be received and expenses when projected to be paid, as
compared to Cash Accounting and Reporting System

AAS   Advanced Accounting System

A general accounting term.

AAT   Association of Accounting Technicians
(aat.org.uk)

The **Association of Accounting Technicians,** is an accountancy
organisation with over 120,000 members worldwide. The AAT
is a technician level qualification which entitles those who have
completed the exams and obtained relevant supervised work
experience to call themselves accountants. The AAT is based in
London but there are branches all over the UK and the rest of the
world.

ABA   Accredited Business Accountant

Accredited Business Advisor
(www.acatcredentials.org)

A professional accounting credential that demonstrates to clients,
potential clients and employers that the credential holder has
a thorough knowledge and proficiency in financial accounting,
financial reporting, financial statement preparation, taxation,
managerial accounting, business law, and ethics for small- to
medium-sized businesses. Most ABA holders do not perform
audits. Generally, they are small business owners themselves.

American Bankers Association
(www.aba.com)

A professional association offering programs, products and services
for the banking community. National source of information and
commentary on banking issues.

American Bar Association
(www.americanbar.org)

A professional association offering programs, products and services
to the legal community. National source of information and
commentary on legal issues.

ABB   Activity-based Budgeting

Is a type of budgeting that involves quantitative explanation of the activities and business processes of the organization with forecasts and financial requirements to achieve target sand corporate goals.

ABC   ## ABC Inventory Analysis or Management, ABC Method, ABC analysis

Inventory control method which categorizes by order of importance (*e.g.*, As are higher-valued items, Bs are lower-valued items and Cs are items with the lowest priority in terms of control and attention. An inventory control system that divides the inventory into three classes. It gives the most attention to A inventory, then B, then C. The figure is an illustration of the ABC inventory control system.

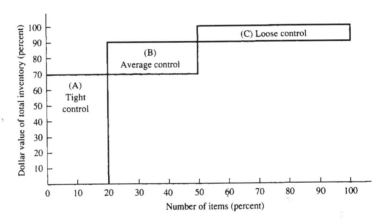

Activity-Based Costing

An accounting framework based on determining the cost of activities and allocating these costs to products, using activity rates. An activity-based cost system is one which first traces costs to activities and then to products. Traditional product costing also involves two stages, but in the first stage costs are traced to departments, not to activities. In both traditional and activity-based costing, the second stage consists of tracing costs to the product. The principal difference between the two methods is the number of cost drivers used. Activity-based costing uses a much larger number of cost drivers than the one or two volume-based cost drivers typical in a conventional system. In fact, the approach separates overhead costs into overhead cost pools, where each cost pool is associated with a different cost driver. Then a predetermined overhead rate is computed for each cost pool and each cost driver. In consequence, this method has enhanced accuracy. Exhibit 1 compares tradition and ABC systems.

Exhibit 1: Cost System Comparison

	Traditional	ABC
Cost pools:	One or a limited Number	Many to reflect different Activated
Applied rate:	Volume-based, Financial	Activity-based, Nonfinancial
Suited for:	Labor-intensive, Low-overhead companies	Capital-intensive, Product-diverse, High-overhead companies
Benefits:	Simple, Inexpensive	Accurate product costing, Possible elimination of Non-value-added activities

Audit Bureau of Circulation

A third-party organization that verifies the circulation of print media through periodic audits.

ABM   ### Activity-Based Management

An advanced control system that focuses management's attention on activities with the objective of improving the value received by the customer and the profit received by providing this value. It includes driver analysis, activity analysis, and performance evaluation and draws on activity-based costing as a major source of information. ABM is a systemwide, integrated approach that focuses management's attention on activities with the goal of improving customer value, reducing costs, and the resulting profit. The basic premise of ABM is: *Products consume activities; activities consume resources.* To be competitive, you must know both (1) the activities that go into manufacturing the products or providing the services, and (2) the cost of those activities. To cut down a product's costs, you will likely have to change the activities the product consumes. An attitude such as "I want across-the-board-cuts—everyone reduce cost by 10%" rarely obtains the desired results.

Automated Banking Machine

Canadian term.

ABS　**Asset-Backed Securities**

Bonds or notes backed by loans or accounts receivable originated by banks, credit card companies or other providers of credit. Brokerage firms that reoffer them to the public underwrite the securities. Also called Pass-Through Securities.

Automated Bond System

Computerized system used by the New York Stock Exchange (NYSE) for recording bids and offers for inactively traded bonds until they are cancelled or executed.

AC　**Actual Cost**

Accounting term for exact amount as opposed to budgeted or expected amount in connection with a given expense.

ACA　**Associate of the Institute of Chartered Accountants in Ireland**

Fully qualified members of Chartered Accountants Ireland earn the designation ACA (Associate Chartered Accountant).

Associate of the Institute of Chartered Accountants in England and Wales
(icaew.com)

The ACA qualification is a world leading professional in accountancy, finance and business

ACAUS **Association of the Association of Chartered Accountants in the US**
(acaus.org)

Association of Chartered Accountants in the U.S. is a professional, nonprofit organization that represents the interests of US based chartered accountants in USA.

ACCA　**Association of Chartered Certified Accountants**
(accaglobal.com)

The global body for professional accountants offering the Chartered Certified Accountant qualification (ACCA or FCCA).

The ACCA is the global body for professional accountants. Their aim is to offer business-relevant, first-choice qualifications to people of application, ability and ambition around the world who seek a rewarding career in accountancy, finance and management

Associate of the Association of Chartered Certified Accountants

Fellowship, or senior membership of ACCA, is awarded automatically based on 5 years' continuous membership, subject to compliance with Continuing Professional Development requirements.*http://en.wikipedia.org/wiki/Association_of_Chartered_Certified_Accountants – cite_note-3*. Fellow members of ACCA use the designatory letters FCCA in place of ACCA

ACE   Automated Commercial Environment

A US Customs electronic data system, which provides support for enforcing trade and contraband laws, ensuring trade compliance, and providing service and information to the international trade community. When completed, it will cover the full gamut of Customs activities.

ACES   Advanced Computerized Execution System

System run by the National Association of Securities Dealers (NASD), which owns and operates the National Association of Securities Dealers Automated Quotation System (NASDAQ).

ACIArb   Associate of the Chartered Institute of Arbitrators

Associates, are entitled to use the designation "ACIArb" after their names

ACIB   Associate of the Chartered Institute of Bankers

Now known as the ifs School of Finance. Chartered Associateship is a professional designation awarded to experienced Alumni Members who have successfully completed an ifs degree or Associateship qualification and undertaken a programme of monitored Continuing Professional Development

ACII   Associate of the Chartered Insurance Institute

Member holding the Advanced Diploma in Insurance

ACMA   Associate of the Chartered Institute of Management Accountants

ACRS Accelerated Cost Recovery System; Accelerated Capital Recovery System

Accounting and tax term concerning rules for depreciation of certain types of assets and property. The Economic Recovery Tax Act of 1981 made the cost of assets purchased after 1980 recoverable at an accelerated rate under the ACRS. *See also* **ADR; MACRS**.

AcSEC Accounting Standards Executive Committee

Committee of the American Institute of CPAs that issues standards, regulations and guidelines for the accounting profession.

ACSI American Consumer Satisfaction Index
(www.theacsi.org)

A U.S. model which tracks consumer satisfaction with a range of products and services across a wide group of industries, developed jointly the American Society for Quality Control and the University of Michigan Business School. The ACSI model is a cause-and-effect model with indices for drivers of satisfaction on the left side (customer expectations, perceived quality, and perceived value), satisfaction (ACSI) in the center, and outcomes of satisfaction on the right side (customer complaints and customer loyalty, including customer retention and price tolerance).

ACU Asian Currency Unit

A unit of a Singaporean bank that deals in foreign currency deposits and loans.

ACV Actual Cash Value

The common method of determining the amount of reimbursement for a loss. Replacement cost less depreciation.

AD&D Accidental Death and Dismemberment

A type of health insurance that pays a lump sum if the insured is accidentally killed in an auto accident or if he/she is hit by another car. The policy also pays a portion of the insured amount if he/she loses part of his/her body such as a leg, an arm or an eye. It may also pay disability income should he/she become totally disabled.

ADB Adjusted Debit Balance

Accounting and banking term to indicate revision or adjustment made based on generally accepted accounting principles (**GAAP**).

Asian Development Bank

(www.adb.org)

A multilateral development bank, dedicated to reducing poverty in Asia and the Pacific region through inclusive economic growth, environmentally sustainable growth, and regional integration.

ADEA Age Discrimination in Employment Act

The 1967 legislation that prohibits job discrimination against people age 40 and older. It prohibits discrimination in pay, benefits, and continued employment. ADEA outlaws almost all mandatory retirement. It awards *double unpaid wages* for willful violations, and grants a broad set of private lawsuit remedies.

ADR Advance Determination Ruling

Ruling issued by the Internal Revenue Service (**IRS**).

American Depository Receipt

A certificate of ownership, issued by a U.S. bank, representing a claim on underlying foreign stocks. ADRs let U.S. residents buy and sell foreign stocks without the hassle of actually owning them. Banks issue ADRs, not the corporation's stock certificate, to an American investor who buys shares of that corporation. Shareholders are entitled to dividends and capital gains. The stock certificate is kept at the bank. The Bank of New York maintains indexes of how ADRS listed in the United States perform. This information can be retrieved at the Bank of New York Internet site *(http://www.adrbnymellon.com/home_dr.jsp)*. J.P.Morgan also maintains an Internet site providing ADR market performance *(www.adr.com)*. You can download *The Complete Depository Receipt (DR) Directory* from the Bank of New York Website.

Asset Depreciation Range system

Internal Revenue Service (IRS) system of guidelines that establish recommended ranges of depreciation to be applied to various classes of assets. *Also see* **ACRS**.

Automatic Dividend Reinvestment

An investment term for a program in which dividends are directly reinvested rather than paid out periodically to the investor. This allows investors to accumulate capital over the long term using "dollar cost averaging" (also referred to as constant dollar plan), which allows investors to invest a fixed amount of dollars at specified times. Thus, more shares are bought when the price is low and fewer shares are bought when the price is high.

ADS   Annual Debt Service

Accounting term for total annual amount paid by an investor in connection with a long-term loan (*e.g.*, mortgage).

AEOSP All Employee Share Option Scheme

Employee share schemes that allow all employees to share in the success of that company

AFAANZ
Accounting and Finance Association of Australia and New Zealand

(afaanz.org)

AFAANZ is the premier body representing the interests of accounting and finance academics and other persons interested in accounting and finance education and research in Australia and New Zealand.

AI   Artificial Intelligence

A computer software program that imitates human intelligence and learning from experience. AI performs complex strategies that assist in determining the best or worst way to accomplish a task or avoid problems. AI programming languages include PROLOG, OPS5, POPLOG, ESIE, LISP and INTERLISP, a version of LISP

AI applications include:

- Financial ratio analysis
- Management services
- Tax planning and preparation
- Planning and audit analysis
- Analyzing accounts receivable

Some AI programs include:

- *Taxadvisor* developed by R. Michaelson, University of Illinois. This program is used for estate planning.
- *Auditor* developed by C. Dungan, University of Illinois. This package is for examining bad debts.

AICPA   American Institute of Certified Public Accountants
(www.aicpa.org)

The professional association of Certified Public Accountants (CPAs). It is a group of accountants who issue pronouncements which make up Generally Accepted Accounting Principles (GAAP). The AICPA also issues Statements on Auditing Standards, which set forth the requirements to be followed by independent CPAs when conducting audits of their clients' financial statements.

AID   Agency for International Development
(www.usaid.gov)

An organization providing and supporting funding and education from the U.S. to emerging nations.

AIM   Alternative Investment Market (UK)

Is a sub-market of the London Stock Exchange, allowing companies to float shares with a less demanding regulatory system than is required by the main market.

AIS   Accounting Information System

Subsystem of Management Information System (*see* **MIS**) that comprises the activities involved in the preparation of financial information, and the information obtained from transactions for both internal and external reporting.

AISG   Accountant International Study Group

An organization that studied the differences in accounting practices between various countries. The Accountant International Study Group was formed in 1966 by professionals from Canada, the United Kingdom and the United States. By 1973, the group expanded its membership to include international accounting standards. The group then folded into the International Accounting Standards Committee (IASC) in 1973, which was reorganized under the International Federation of Accountants and eventually became the International Accounting Standards Board (**IASB**).

AITD   All Inclusive Trust Deed

A mortgage (trust deed) that encompasses existing mortgages and is subordinate (junior) to them; also called *wraparound mortgage*. The existing mortgages stay on the property and the new mortgage wraps around them. The excising mortgage loan generally carries

A

lower interest rates than the one on the new mortgage loan. This loan arrangement is a form of seller financing.

ALC   Accelerated Loan Commitment

Accounting and banking term for voluntary acceleration of payments by a borrower, generally to decrease interest payments over the life of the loan.

AMA   Asset Management Account

Investment term for a type of account that provides a variety or menu of investment and financial management and planning services with the objective of centralizing several of an investor's needs within one organization.

American Management Association
(www.amanet.org)

An association of executives, managers, and supervisors in industry, commerce, government, and nonprofit organizations. It is a global not-for-profit, membership-based association that provides a full range of management development and educational services to individuals, companies and government agencies worldwide, including 486 of the Fortune 500 companies. Each year, thousands of business professionals acquire the latest business know-how, valuable insights and increased confidence at AMA seminars, conferences, current issues forums and briefings, as well as through AMA books and publications, research and print and online self-study courses.

American Marketing Association
(www.marketingpower.com)

An international professional organization for people involved in the practice, study and teaching of marketing. Its principal roles are: (1) to always understand and satisfy the needs of marketers so as to provide them with products and services that will help them be better marketers, (2) to empower marketers through information, education, (3) provide relationships and resources that will enrich their professional development and careers., and (4) to advance the thought, application and ethical practice of marketing.

AMBAC American Municipal Bond Assurance Corporation

U.S. Government oversight organization involved with municipal bond issues.

AMEX   American Stock Exchange
(www.nyse.com)

Acquired by NYSE Euronext (NYX) in 2008, the world's leading and most diverse exchange group, the third-largest stock exchange by trading volume in the United States and now the NYSE Amex Equities in 2009. This exchange handles about 10% of all securities traded in the U.S. Today, almost all trading on the exchange is in small-cap stocks, exchange-traded funds (ETFs) and derivatives.

AMI   Alternative Mortgage Instruments

A generic descriptive term for mortgage financing other than conventional lenders.

AMPS   Auction Market Preferred Stock

Type of adjustable-rate preferred stock on which the dividend is determined every seven weeks in an auction process in which the price is gradually lowered until it meets a responsive bid from a corporate bidder.

AMS   Agricultural Marketing Service

A service of the United States government which assures purchasers of U.S. goods that they satisfy quality standards and contractual commitments.

AMT   Alternative Minimum Tax

A U.S. IRS mechanism created to ensure that high-income individuals, corporations, trusts, and estates pay at least some minimum amount of tax, regardless of deductions, credits or exemptions. It operates by adding certain tax-preference items back into adjusted gross income. It is taxed based in part on the taxpayer's tax preferences that is levied when it exceeds the regular tax. The idea behind the AMT is that everyone should pay a fair share of taxes.

AMVI   AMEX Market Value Index

One of two major market indexes compiled by the American Stock Exchange. An unweighted index of AMEX stocks, computed as the sum of all of the plus net changes, minus net changes above or below previous closing prices. This sum is divided by the number of issues listed, and the result added to or subtracted from the previous close.

AON   All or None

In investment banking, an offering in which the issuer has the right to cancel the entire issue if the underwriting is not fully subscribed. In securities, a buy or sell order marked to signify that no partial transaction is to be executed.

A/P   Accounts Payable

Accounting term for bill payment systems and processes.

APACS Association for Payment Clearing Services

Is a United Kingdom trade organization that brings together all payment systems organizations. Now called The UK Payments Administration Ltd.

APAS   Advance Pricing Agreement

An agreement between the internal revenue service and a taxpayer on the acceptability of a transfer price. The agreement is private and is binding on both parties for a specified period of time.

APB   Accounting Practice Bulletin

One of a series of bulletins published by the Financial Accounting Standards Board (FASB) giving accountants guidance in applying Generally Accepted Accounting Principles (GAAP) and other rules and standards to new or unfamiliar situations.

Auditing Practices Board

The Auditing Practices Board Limited was originally established in 1991 as a committee of the Consultative Committee of Accountancy Bodies, to take responsibility within both Ireland and the United Kingdom for setting standards of auditing with the objective of enhancing public confidence in the audit process and the quality and relevance of audit services in the public interest. In 2002 APB was re-established under the auspices of The Accountancy Foundation and, following a UK government review, it has been transferred to the Financial Reporting Council.

Accounting Principles Board

Former body of AICPA that used to determine accounting procedures and principles for the accounting field. The APB was replaced by the financial Accounting Standards Board (FASB).

APICS American Production And Inventory Control Society
(www.apics.org)

An international, not-for-profit organization serving the manufacturing, materials management, resource management, and service industries. Established in 1957, American Production and Inventory Control Society (APICS) is designed to meet the needs of professionals in all areas of resource management, including inventory, materials, information systems, accounting/finance, supply chain, and all other functional areas that contribute to the overall efficiency and productivity of an organization.

APM Arbitrage Pricing Model

A pricing model that includes multiple risk factors, besides the security's *beta*. This is in contrast to the Capital Asset Pricing Model (CAPM), which assumes that required rates of return depend only on one risk factor, the stock's *beta*. APM maintains that security returns vary from their expected amounts when there are unanticipated changes in basic economic forces. Such forces would include unexpected changes in industrial production, inflation rates, term structure of interest rates, and the difference between interest rates of high-and-low risk bonds.

APR Annual Percentage Rate

1. A true measure of the effective cost of credit. It is the ratio of the finance charge to the average amount of credit in use during the life of the loan, and is expressed as a percentage rate per year. Assume Sharon took out a $1,000,000, one year, 10% discounted loan to buy real estate. The effective interest rate equals: $100,000/ ($1,000,000 – $100,000) = $100,000/$900,000 = 11%. In this discount loan, the proceeds received is only $900,000, which effectively increases the cost of the loan.

2. The effective annual yield, also called the *annual percentage yield (APY)*. Different types of investments use different compounding periods. For example, most bonds pay interest semiannually. Some banks pay interest quarterly. If an investor wishes to compare investments with different compounding periods, he needs to put them on a common basis. The annual percentage rate (APR), or effective annual rate, is used for this purpose and is computed as follows:

    $$APR = (1 + r/m)^m - 1.0$$

    where r = the stated, nominal or quoted rate

    m = the number of compounding periods per year.

Example

Assume that a bank offers 6 percent interest, compounded quarterly, then the APR is:

APR= $(1 + .06/4)^4 - 1.0 = (1.015)^4 - 1.0 = 1.0614 - 1.0 = .0614 = .0614 = 6.14\%$

This means that if one bank offered 6 percent with quarterly compounding, while another offered 6.14 percent with annual compounding, they would both be paying the same effective rate of interest.

APY   Annual Percentage Yield

See **APR.**

AQL   Acceptable Quality Level

A predetermined level of defective products that a company permits to be sold.

A/R   Accounts Receivable

Accounting term for systems and processes connected with payments owed to the organization.

ARM   Adjustable Rate Mortgage

Mortgage (generally residential) for which the interest rate will be adjusted at certain pre-specified times during the life of the loan, based on prevailing indices at the time of adjustment, and generally also carrying pre-specified limits on the percentage by which the interest rate can increase. Also called Variable Rate Mortgages and Flexible Rate Mortgages.

ARPS   Adjustable Rate Preferred Stock

Preferred stock whose dividend is adjusted based on changes in the Treasury bill rate or other money market rate, generally quarterly.

ARR   Accounting Rate of Return

Also called *simple rate of return.* Measures profitability from a conventional accounting point of view. ARR relates the required investment to the future annual net income. Rule of thumb: Select the project with the highest ARR. The formula is:

$$ARR = \frac{Cash\ inflows - straight\ line\ depreciation}{Initial\ investment}$$

Assume the following:

Initial investment	$20,000
Estimated life of investment	20 years
Cash inflows per year	$3,000
Straight line depreciation	$600

$$ARR = \frac{\$3,000 - \$600}{\$20,000} = 0.12\% \times 100 = 12\%$$

Then:

The average investment is usually assumed to be one-half of the original investment. Thus, in this case, the investment amount is decreased each year by $600 and the ARR is computed by one-half of the original cost. Thus, the ARR is doubled as follows:

$$ARR = \frac{\$3,000 - \$600}{1/2\ \$20,000} = \frac{\$2,400}{\$10,000} = 0.24\% \times 100 = 24\%$$

Disadvantage:

1. Does not take into account the time value of money
2. Uses accounting rather than cash flow information.

ARS   Auction-Rate Security

An auction of a corporate or municipal bond, which finances items such as infrastructure, schools, general municipal expenditures, or refunding of old debt. Investors such as municipalities, colleges, or other institutions who desire to acquire an ARS submit bids in an auction.

ARSC   Accounting and Review Services Committee

Committee under the American Institute of CPAs.

ASB   Auditing Standards Board

The senior technical body of the American Institute of CPAs, designated to issue pronouncements on auditing matters.

ASCII   American Standard Code for Information Interchange

A standard code for conversion of characters to a binary number so that they are understandable by many microcomputers.

ASP **American Selling Price**

For customs purposes, the price used as a tax base for determining import duties.

ASPCA Australian Society of Certified Practising Accountants

ASPIRIN
Australian Stock Price Riskless Indexed Notes

Investment instrument.

ASX **Australia Stock Exchange**

(www.asx.com.au)

ATAR **Awareness-Trial-Availability-Repeat Model**

A model that projects future sales growth without data. The ATAR model originates from what is called *diffusion of innovation,* explained this way: for a person or a firm to become a regular buyer/user of an innovation, there must first be awareness that it exists, then there must be a decision to try that innovation, then the person must find the item available to them, and finally there must be the type of happiness with it that leads to adoption, or repeat usage.

ATM **Automatic Teller Machine**

An automated or automatic teller machine (ATM) (American, Australian and UK), also known as an automated banking machine (**ABM**) (Canadian).

ATP **Advanced Technology Products**

Products whose technology is from a recognized high technology field, represent leading edge technology in that field, and constitute a significant part of all items covered in the selected classification code.

Arbitrage Trading Program

Investment banking program involving the simultaneous purchase and sale or exchange of securities or commodities in different (sometimes foreign) markets to profit from unequal prices. Also known as program trading.

AUD **Australian Dollar**

Currency of Australia

AuSB   Auditing Standards Board (Canada)

AWSCPA
American Woman's Society of Certified Public Accountants
(www.awscpa.org)

A national organization dedicated to serving all women CPAs. The AWSCPA provides a supportive environment and valuable resources for members to achieve their personal and professional goals through various opportunities including leadership, networking and education.

B

BA Banker's Acceptance

A time draft drawn by a business firm whose payment is guaranteed by the bank's "acceptance" of it. It is especially important in foreign trade, when the seller of goods can be certain that the buyer's draft will actually have funds behind it. Banker's acceptances are money market instruments actively traded in the secondary market.

BACS Bankers Automated Clearing Services

Is a United Kingdom scheme for the electronic processing of financial transactions.

B&F Business and Farm

Banking descriptor for a particular type of property.

BAL, BALCE
Balance

BAN Bond Anticipation Note

Short-term debt investment instrument issued by a municipality or state. Issues are paid off with the returns from a bond issue.

BATNA Best Alternative to Negotiated Agreement

BBB Better Business Bureau

(www.bbb.org)

Local business supported organizations that maintain records on local business firms and provide information to concerned consumers. Local bureaus are part of a loosely tied national system.

BBS Bulletin Board System

1. A collection of message boards and files devoted to a particular topic.
2. Properly known as the OTC *Bulletin Board*, an electronic quotation service that lists the prices of stocks that do not meet the minimum requirements for listing on a stock exchange or the Nasdaq stock-listing system.

B

BC   **Bad Check** or **Bogus Check**

Banking term for a check uncollectable because either the account has insufficient funds or the check itself is fraudulent.

BCG Matrix
Boston Consulting Group Growth-Share Matrix

A strategy tool, developed by the Boston Consulting Group (BCG), to guide resource allocation decisions on the basis of growth and market share of a company's strategic business units (SBUs). The BCG growth-share matrix defines four business groups:

- Cash cows (low growth, high market share)
- Stars (high growth, high market share)
- Question marks (high growth, low market share)
- Dogs (low growth, low market share)

BCP   **Budget Change Proposal**

General business and accounting document for submitting a request for a revision to an existing budget or business plan.

BD   **Bank Draft**

Banking term for conventional paper check.

BDI   **Basic Defense Interval**

A stringent measure of liquidity. The BDI is calculated: (Cash + Receivables + Marketable Securities) / ((Operating Expenses + Interest + Income Taxes)/365).

B/E   **Bill of Exchange**

Also called a draft, an order written by an exporter instructing an importer or an importer's agent such as a bank to pay a specified amount of money at a specified time. The individual or business initiating the bill of exchange is called the maker, while the party to whom the bill is presented is called the drawee.

B/E, B-E Break-Even Point

General business term for number of units at which total variable and fixed costs connected with a program, product or service, are equal to revenue from sales of the same number of units, and beyond which sales begin to produce a profit (see Exhibit 1 below).

B

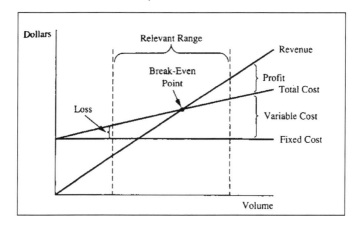

BEA   Break-Even Analysis

An analytical technique used to determine the level of output needed to be produced so that the firm covers both all of its variable costs and fixed costs; also called *cost-volume-profit (CVP) analysis*. Relationships among the firm's cost structure, volume of output including the mix, and earnings are studied. The analysis tries to answer the following questions:

(a) What sales volume is required to break even?

(b) What sales volume is necessary to earn a desired profit?

(c) What profit can be expected on a given sales volume?

(d) How would changes in selling price, variable costs, fixed costs, and output affect profits?

(e) How would a change in the mix of products sold affect the break-even and target income volume and profit potential?

BF   Bankruptcy Fee

Australian finance term.

Brought Forward

Accounting term for amount carried from one time period to another.

BFC   Budget and Forecast Calendarization

Accounting and general business term for allocating an annual budget across smaller time periods (quarterly or monthly).

B

BFCY   Beneficiary

Insurance term for the designated person to receive the benefits of an insurance policy upon the demise of the insured.

BFOQ   Bona Fide Occupational Qualification

Concerning a Title VII employment discrimination complaint, a defense based on the qualifications that the employer requires in order for the employee to perform a job.

BFY   Budget Fiscal Year

Accounting and general business term for the dates on which an entity's financial year begins and ends (*e.g.*, Jan. 1 through Dec. 31, or July 1 through June 30).

BIC   Bank Investment Contract

A bank-guaranteed interest in a portfolio providing a specified yield over a specified period of time.

Business Identifier Codes

Is a unique identification code for both financial and non-financial institutions

BIN   Bank Identification Number

U.S. banking term for number unique to each institution used for automated processing efficiencies.

BIP   Bureau of International Programs

An agency of the U.S. Department of Commerce.

BKCY; BKY
Bankruptcy

Banking and general business term for the condition of being adjudged financially insolvent.

BKG; BKPG
Bookkeeping

General business term for keeping account books.

B/L   Bill of Lading

A time draft drawn by a multinational company whose payment

is guaranteed by the bank's "acceptance" of it. It is especially important in international trade, when the seller of goods can be certain that the buyer's draft will actually have funds behind it. Banker's acceptances are money market instruments actively traded in the secondary market.

BLS **Bureau of Labor Statistics**
(www.bls.gov)

U.S. Department of Commerce agency. It is the principal Federal agency responsible for measuring labor market activity, working conditions, and price changes in the economy. Its mission is to collect, analyze, and disseminate essential economic information to support public and private decision-making. As an independent statistical agency, BLS serves its diverse user communities by providing products and services that are objective, timely, accurate, and relevant.

BMIR **Below-Market Interest Rate**

Banking and general business term for lending terms below prevailing rates for similar loans.

B/O **Back-Order; Back-Ordered**

General business term for goods out of stock and waiting to be replenished.

BOE **Board of Equalization**

A governmental body that reviews property tax assessment procedures.

BOM **Beginning of the Month**

Accounting and banking term used as indicator for commencement of accounting period or date on which a given financial transaction is scheduled.

Bill of Materials

A listing of all the assemblies, sub-assemblies, parts, and raw materials that are needed to produce one unit of a finished product. Each finished product has its own bill of materials.

BOMA **Building Owners and Managers Association**
(www.boma.org)

A Washington, D.C.-based organization with subsidiaries

B

throughout U.S., providing programs, products and services to individuals and organizations providing commercial and multi-unit residential property management services.

BOP   Balance of Payments

A systematic record of a country's receipts from, or payments to, other countries. In a way, it is like the balance sheets for businesses, only on a national level. The reference you see in the media to the *balance of trade* usually refers to goods within the goods and services category of the current account. It is also known as *merchandise* or *"visible" trade* because it consists of tangibles like foods, manufactured goods, and raw materials. "Services," the other part of the category, is known as "invisible" trade and consists of intangibles such as interest or dividends, technology transfers, and others (like insurance, transportation, and financial). When the net result of both the current account and the capital account yields more credits than debits, the country is said to have a surplus in its balance of payments. Figures are reported in seasonally adjusted volumes and dollar amounts. It is the only non-survey, non-judgmental report that appears in *Survey of Current Business* produced by the *Department of Commerce*.

BOQ   Beginning of Quarter

Accounting term for first date of a given fiscal quarter.

BOVESPA
   Bolsa de Valores de Sao Paulo

Largest of Brazil's nine stock exchanges.

BOY   Beginning of Year

Accounting and general business term for the commencement of a new fiscal year.

BPR   Business Process Reengineering

An approach aiming at making revolutionary changes as opposed to evolutionary changes by eliminating non-value-added steps in a business process and computerizing the remaining steps to achieve desired outcomes. *See also* **TQM**.

B **BR   Bills Receivable**

Accounting term, similar to Accounts Receivable.

BRE **Business Reply Envelope**

General business term for postage-paid return envelopes, often used to increase response rate in direct-mail marketing campaigns and as a customer-service feature.

BRL **Brazilian Real**

Currency of Brazil

BS **Balance Sheet**

Accounting and general business term for a document that summarizes an organization's financial condition on a given date.

Bill of Sale

General business term for documentation for a purchase or sale of goods.

BSC **Balanced Scorecard**

A strategic-based performance management system that typically identifies objectives and measures for four different perspectives: the financial perspective, the customer perspective, the process perspective, and the learning and growth perspective. A variety of potential measures for each perspective of a Balanced Scorecard are indicated in the figure below.

Balanced scorecard

Perspective	Issue	Measures
Financial	Is the company achieving its financial goals?	Operating income Return on assets Sales growth Cash flow from operations Reduction of administrative expense
Customer	Is the company meeting customer expectations?	Customer satisfaction Customer retention New customer acquisition Market share On-time delivery Time to fill orders

B

Processes	Is the company improving critical internal processes?	Defect rate Lead time Number of suppliers Material turnover Percent of practical capacity
Learning and Growth	Is the company improving its ability to innovate?	Amount spent on employee training Employee satisfaction Employee retention Number of new products New product sales as a percent of total sales Number of patents

BSD   **Bahamian Dollar**

Currency of the Bahamas

BSE   **Bombay Stock Exchange**

Boston Stock Exchange

Brussels Stock Exchange

BSI   **British Standards Institution**

Is the business standards company whose principal activity is the production of standards for businesses as part of their everyday activities.

B2B   **Business-to-Business E-Commerce**

The online selling of goods and services between businesses. Using B2B trading networks, auction sites, spot exchanges, online product catalogs, barter sites, and other online resources to reach new customers, this online business serves current business customers more effectively, and obtains buying efficiencies and better prices.

B2C   **Business-to-Consumer E-Commerce**

The online selling of goods and services to final customers.

B

BTR   **Bureau of Trade Regulation**
U.S. Department of Commerce organization.

BY   **Budget Year**
Australian business term for an organization's financial year.

B

C

CA **Capital Account**

Banking and investment brokerage term for accounts that holds a significant proportion of an organization's or investor's wealth.

Capital Appreciation

Banking term for return on investment of primary capital.

Chartered Accountant

Certification of competency in accounting. Less rigorous than Certified Public Accountant.

Cost Account

Accounting and general business term for account established for direct costs associated with production.

Cost Accountant

Accounting term for personnel responsible for determining costs of items involved in production.

Credit Account

Banking and accounting term for account established in which credit can be drawn up to a specified amount.

Current Account

Banking and Accounting term for account with ongoing activity.

CABNIS
Consortia of American Businesses in the Newly Independent States

U.S. Department of Commerce agency.

CACM **Central American Common Market**

CACPAF
Continental Association of CPA Firms

London-based organization of CPA firms whose members practice and clients exist in both U.S. and Europe.

CAD Cash Against Documents

Accounting term for comparison of current cash assets to long-term and other debt.

Cash against Documents

A transaction where the buyer assumes ownership/title for the goods being purchased upon paying the agreed upon sale price in cash.

Computer-Aided Design

Use of a computer to interact with a designer in developing and testing product ideas without actually building prototypes.

Canadian Dollar

Currency of Canada

CAD/CAM
Computer-Aided Design and Manufacturing

Computerized system to both integrate part design and to generate processing or manufacturing instructions.

CAF; C&F
Cost and Freight

Exporter's quoted price and freight charges to the destination.

CAFR Comprehensive Annual Financial Report

The annual report of a government. The report includes combined and individual balance sheets, as follows:

- All funds: Statement of revenues, expenditures and fund balance changes.
- General and special revenue funds: Statement of revenues, expenditures and fund balance changes.
- Proprietary funds: Statement of revenues, expenditures and retained earnings changes.
- Proprietary funds: Statement of changes in financial position.

CAGR Compound Annual Growth Rate

The year over year growth rate applied to an investment or other part of a company's activities over a multiple-year period; also called *annual percentage rate (APR)*, or *effective annual rate*. The

C

formula for calculating CAGR is $(1 + r/m)^m - 1.0$

where   r= the stated, nominal or quoted rate

m= the number of compounding periods per year.

CAM Computer-Aided Manufacturing

Manufacturing system utilizing computer software that controls the actual machine on the shop floor.

CAP Capitalization Rate

1. A tool used by real estate agents to determine a value of an investment; also called *cap rate* or *income yield*. It is calculated by dividing a property's net operating income (NOI) by its purchase price. That interest rate, which when applied to the earnings of an investment, determines its appraisal or market value. The higher the cap rate, the lower the perceived risk to the investor and the lower the asking price paid. Whether a piece of property is over-priced or not depends on the rate of the similar type property derived from the market place. The method has two limitations: (1) it is based on only the first year's NOI, and (2) it ignores return through appreciation in property value.

2. A concept which relates the proportion of each class of share or debt capital in a firm to its total market capitalization. Many companies of large size issue several classes of shares.

CAPM Capital Asset Pricing Model

This is used to determine a theoretically appropriate required rate of return of an asset

Accounting and banking term for methodologies and guidelines used in setting a value on a capital asset. The CAPM relates the risk measured by beta to the level of expected or required rate of return on a security. Stated as follows:

$$r_j = r_f + b(r_m - r_f)$$

where: r_j is the expected (required) return on security j.

r_f is the risk-free security (*e.g.*, a T-bill)

r_m is the expected return on the market portfolio (*e.g.*, the S&P 500 or the DJIA)

b is an index of non-diversifiable, non-controllable, systematic risk (*e.g.*, Beta).

C

Another option used to measure the cost of a stock using CAPM involves the following considerations:

1. The T-bill, considered the U.S. risk-free rate, rf, is estimated.
2. A stock's beta coefficient, b, an index of systematic (non-diversifiable market) risk is estimated.
3. A rate of return of a market portfolio (*e.g.*, S&P 500) is estimated.
4. The required rate of return on a firm's stock is estimated using the following formula:

$$k_e = r_f + b\,(r_m - r_f)$$

Also called the *security market line (SML)*.

CAPS Convertible Adjustable Preferred Stock

Preferred stock with an adjustable interest rate pegged to Treasury security rates and that can be exchanged, during the period after the announcement of each dividend rate for the next period, for common stock or cash with a market value equal to the par value of the stock.

CAPSR Cost Account Performance Status Report

Accounting term for summary of accuracy in a prior time period of cost projections compared to reality.

CAS Contract Accounting Standard

Accounting term for internally established standard against which a contract price is compared.

CAT Certified Accounting Technician

UK qualification offered by the Association of Chartered Certified Accountants

CATS Certificate of Accrual on Treasury Securities

Investment term for document of accrued earnings on U.S. Treasury securities.

CAV Credit Account Voucher

Banking term for document that indicates the amount of credit available in the stated account on a given date.

C

CB   Cash Book

Accounting term for summary of a cash account.

Credit Balance

Accounting and banking term for amount of credit available in a given account or to a given customer.

C/B   Cost/Benefit

General business term for quantitative and qualitative analysis of factors involved in a proposed venture.

CBA   Certified Business Appraiser

Certification offered by the Institute of Business Appraisers (*www. go-iba.org/professional-certifications/certified-business-appraiser.html*) to those meeting established education and practice standards for appraising the value of a business.

Chartered Bank Auditor

Certification offered by the Bank Administration Institute.

Cost-Benefit Analysis

General business term for quantitative and qualitative analysis of factors involved in a proposed venture.

CBD   Cash Before Delivery

General business term specifying that payment is required before the vendor will make delivery.

Central Business District

Real estate term for densest and generally most desirable area of an urban area, in terms of both office and retail space.

Commerce Business Daily

(www.cbd-net.com)

Publication from the U.S. Department of Commerce, listing proposed government procurements, subcontracting leads and foreign business opportunities. Government agencies are required to announce in the CBD all intended procurements of $25,000 or more, and potential suppliers have at least 30 days to respond.

C

CBE **Cash Break-Even Sales**

Unit or dollar sales volume at which operating cash receipts equal operating cash disbursements.

Certified Bank Examiner

Professional certification by American Bankers Association.

CBO **Collateralized Bond Obligation**

Investment bond backed by a pool of bonds rated BB or lower, generally packaged in high-risk, high-yield issues separated into three tiers of high-, medium- and low-quality collateral.

CBOE **Chicago Board of Options Exchange**

(www.cboe.com)

Organized, national exchange where foreign currency, index, and interest rate options are traded by members for their own accounts and for the accounts of customers.

CBOT **Chicago Board of Trade**

(www.cmegroup.com)

Now, Chicago Mercantile Exchange (CME). It is the world's largest exchange for futures contracts, in terms of the number of contracts traded (243 million in 1997). Founded in 1848, CBOT trades both financial and commodity futures and futures options. U.S. Treasury bond futures are the most frequently traded instruments. Its big rival is the Chicago Mercantile Exchange, which is particularly strong in agricultural futures contracts.

CBS **Consolidated Balance Sheet**

Abbreviated summary of an organization's financial condition as of a given date.

CCA **Current Cost Accounting**

An accounting calculation that provides more realistic values by valuing assets at current replacement cost, rather than the amount actually paid for them

CCH **Commerce Clearing House**

(www.cch.com)

U.S. publisher of authoritative texts on tax law, accounting and other business subjects.

CCP   **Cost Control Program**

General business term for an initiative undertaken by a business to institute changes directed at reducing costs, generally without affecting production output or quality.

CD   **Certificate of Deposit**

Special type of time deposit. A CD is an investment instrument, available at financial institutions, that generally offers a fixed rate of return for a specified period. The depositor agrees not to withdraw funds until the CD matures. If the funds are withdrawn, a significant penalty is charged. The fixed rate of return normally increases with the amount or the term of the investment.

CDA   **Common Dollar Accounting; Constant Dollar Accounting**

Australian accounting terms.

CDS   **Credit-Default Swap**

A contract or insurance policy between a seller (a bank) and a buyer (bondholder). In this swap, the seller agrees to pay the buyer in the event of a bond default or bankruptcy.

CE   **Capital Expenditure**

Accounting and general business term for purchase of a tangible asset.

Cash Earnings

Accounting and banking term for actual earnings not reinvested and readily available for other uses.

Cost Effectiveness

General business term for concept of soundness of plans and practices based on direct and indirect costs vs. income.

CEBS   **Certified Employee Benefits Specialist**

A professional designation for employee benefit specialists.

CEO   **Chief Executive Officer**

Officer of a firm or organization responsible for its activities, sometimes used as an additional title by the President, Chairman of the Board, Executive Vice President or other officer.

C

CEP   Capital Expenditure Proposal

General business term for proposition that involves a business making a major investment in, *e.g.*, equipment or real estate in order to enable a new venture.

CF   Carried Forward

Accounting term for applying an expense from one time period to another.

CFA   Cash-Flow Accounting

Accounting system that considers only cash and does not deduct non-cash items such as depreciation.

Cash Flow Analysis

Accounting term for financial analysis that considers only cash and does not consider non-cash items such as depreciation.

Chartered Financial Analyst

Professional certification from the Association for Investment Management and Research. The CFA is awarded to those who pass a rigorous three-level exam covering investment principles, asset valuation and portfolio management, and have at least three years of investment management experience.

CFAT   Cash Flow After Taxes

Accounting term for income less expenses (direct and indirect) and taxes.

CFBT   Cash Flow Before Taxes

Accounting term for income less expenses (direct and indirect).

CFC   Cash Flow Component

Accounting term for a type or category of income or expense within a cash flow statement or analysis.

CFD   Corporate Finance Director

Common job title for a corporate officer responsible for financial planning and recordkeeping.

CFE   Certified Financial Examiner

Professional certification from the Society of Financial Examiners.

CFO   Chief Financial Officer

Common job title for a corporate officer responsible for handling funds, signing checks over a certain amount, financial planning and recordkeeping.

CFP   Certified Financial Planner

A professional designation conferred upon those candidates who demonstrate a high level of skill and competence in the analysis of client financial conditions and the development of client-oriented personal financial plans by passing a series of national examinations administered by the College for Financial Planning, Denver, Colorado. The CFP program consists of six separate parts, each of which is a three-hour written examination. The program includes the following parts: (1) introduction to financial planning; (2) risk management; (3) investments; (4) tax planning and management; (5) retirement planning and employee benefits; and (6) estate planning. The candidates must also meet other educational and work experience requirements of the College in order to obtain the right to use the College's designation of Certified Financial Planner (CFP).

CFR   Cost and Freight

The seller must pay the costs of bringing the goods to the specified port. The buyer is responsible for risks when the goods are loaded onto the ship.

CFRM   Contract Financial Reporting Manual

Documentation for a business' systems to maintain compliance with vendor and other contracts.

CFTC   Commodities Futures Trading Commission

(www.cftc.gov)

Independent agency created by Congress to regulate the U.S. commodity futures and options markets, and to ensure market integrity and protect market participants against manipulation, abusive trade practices, and fraud.

CFY   Company Fiscal Year

Accounting and general business term referring to the calendar by which a business' fiscal year begins and ends.

C

Current Fiscal Year

Accounting and general business term designating an event as occurring during the present financial accounting year.

CG **Capital Gain**

Accounting and tax term for the difference between the amount paid for an investment and the amount received for it when it is sold, when that amount is positive.

CGI **Common Gateway Interface**

Means of programming web sites. Script programs are run on the server. This is different from Java which runs on the client. CGI is primarily used to handle online forms. CGI allows web applications . to be written and executed on multiple different web servers.

CGM **Cost of Goods Manufactured**

The total cost of goods completed during the current period. *See also* CGS.

CGMA **Chartered Global Management Accountant**
(www.cgma.com)

A certificate be offered by AICPA and CIMA Joint Venture to develop and promote a new global management accounting designation.

CGS **Cost of Goods Sold**

Price of purchasing of producing a product that is sold; also called *cost of sales.* Sales less cost of sales equals gross margin (profit). Merchandising organizations, such as Wal-Mart, Rite Aid, and Office Depot, purchase products that are ready for resale. These organizations maintain one inventory account, called Merchandise Inventory, which reflects the costs of products held for resale. To calculate the cost of goods sold for a merchandising organization, the equation is used:

	Beginning	Net Cost	Ending
Cost of Goods Sold =	Merchandise Inventory	+ of Purchase	− Merchandise Inventory

For example, Allison Candy Store had a balance of $3,000 in the Merchandise Inventory account on January 1, 20x0. During the year, the store purchased candy products totalling $23,000 (adjusted for purchase discounts, purchases returns

C

and allowances, and freight-in). At December 31,20x0, the Merchandise Inventory balance was $4,500. The cost of goods sold is thus $21,500.

Cost of Goods Sold = $3,000 + $23,000 − $4,500 = $21,500

Manufacturing firms, such as Nokia, GM, and IBM, use materials, labor, and manufacturing overhead to manufacture products for sale. Materials are purchased and used in the production process. The Materials Inventory account shows the balance of the cost of unused materials. During the production process, the costs of manufacturing the product are accumulated in the Work in Process Inventory account. The balance of the Work in Process Inventory account represents the costs of unfinished product. Once the product is complete and ready for sale, the cost of the goods manufactured is reflected in the Finished Goods Inventory account. The balance in the Finished Goods Inventory account is the cost of unsold completed product. When the product is sold, the manufacturing organization calculates the cost of goods sold using the following equation:

$$\text{Cost of Goods Sold} = \begin{array}{c}\text{Beginning}\\\text{Finished}\\\text{Goods}\\\text{Inventory}\end{array} + \begin{array}{c}\text{Cost of}\\\text{Goods}\\\text{Manufactured}\end{array} - \begin{array}{c}\text{Ending}\\\text{Finished}\\\text{Goods}\\\text{Inventory}\end{array}$$

CHAPS Clearing House Automated Payment System

It is a same-day automated payment system for processing payments made within the UK. It is primarily used for very high value payments and is used by corporates who make large numbers of these payments but it can be used by individuals too

CHF Swiss Franc

Currency of Switzerland

ChFC Chartered Financial Consultant

Financial planning professional designation awarded by the American College of the American Society of Chartered Life Underwriters. Requirements include successful completion of a ten-course program and three years' professional experience.

CHIPS Clearinghouse Interbank Payment System

A computerized clearing network systems for transfer of international dollar payments and settlement of interbank foreign exchange obligations.

C

CI   **Cash Item**

Accounting term for income received or payment made in cash as opposed to securities or other obligations.

Continuous Improvement

Never-ending effort for improvement in every part of the firm relative to all of its deliverables to its customers; also called *Kaizen* in Japanese. It covers improvement of machinery, materials, labor utilization, and production methods through application of suggestions and ideas of team members.

CIA   **Certified Internal Auditor**
(www.theiia.org/certification/certified-internal-auditor)

An accountant certified to possess the professional qualifications of an internal auditor. It is the only globally accepted certification for internal auditors and remains the standard by which individuals demonstrate their competency and professionalism in the internal auditing field. Candidates leave the program enriched with educational experience, information, and business tools that can be applied immediately in any organization or business environment. The CIA exam is also broader than the CPA exam because it covers a broader range of areas, among them management, economics, finance, and quantitative methods. The CIA exam lasts 14 hours (four 3 1/2-hour parts) and covers the following areas:

Part 1 – The Internal Audit Activity's Role in Governance, Risk, and Control

Part 2 – Conducting the Internal Audit Engagement

Part 3 – Business Analysis and Information Technology

Part 4 – Business Management Skills

CIB   **Chartered Institute of Bankers England and Wales**

Now renamed the *ifs* School of Finance

CIC   **Chartered Investment Counselor**

Designation from the Investment Counsel Association of America (Washington D.C.), to those holding CFAs and currently working as investment counselors.

C

CIF   **Corporate Income Fund**

Unit Investment Trust with a fixed portfolio of high-grade securities and other instruments, generally paying income to the investor on a monthly basis.

Cost, Insurance and Freight

The seller must pay the costs of bringing the goods to the specified port. They also pay for insurance. The buyer is responsible for risks when the goods are loaded onto the ship.

CII   **Chartered Insurance Institute**

(cii.co.uk)

The CII is the world's leading professional organisation for insurance and financial services. Its 112,000 members are committed to maintaining the highest standards of technical competence and ethical conduct

CIM   **Computer-Integrated Manufacturing**

Computer information systems utilizing a shared manufacturing database for engineering design, factory production, and information management.

CIMA   **Chartered Institute of Management Accountants**

(www.cimaglobal.com)

The London-based professional body of management accountants. It has 183,000 members and students in 168 countries.

CIMC   **Certified Investment Management Consultant**

Designation from the Institute for Investment Management Consultants (based in Washington D.C., and Phoenix) to members who pass an examination and have at least three years of professional financial consulting experience.

CIMS   **Certified Investment Management Specialist**

Designation from the Institute for Investment Management Consultants (based in Washington D.C., and Phoenix) to associate members who pass an examination and meet financial services work experience requirements.

CIO   **Chief Information Officer**

The title of the top manager of the IT department. He/she is accountable for IT advocacy, aligning IT and business strategies, and planning, resourcing and managing the delivery of IT services, information and the deployment of associated human resources. Other titles include *vice president of information services, director of information services,* and *director of computer services.*

Chief Investment Officer

An executive who is responsible for managing and monitoring the company's investment portfolio. His/her responsibilities include: investment portfolio management, investing surplus funds, pension monies management, maintaining liaison with the investment community, and counseling with financial analysts.

CIOBS   Chartered Institute of Bankers in Scotland

Now trading as The Chartered Banker Institute, is the oldest banking institute in the world and the only remaining banking institute in the UK. They are unique in being entitled to award the "Chartered Banker" designation to their qualified members.

CIOT   Chartered Institute of Taxation

The leading professional body in the United Kingdom concerned solely with taxation.

CIP   Capital Investment Program

General business term for long-term plan for investing capital to meet specific objectives.

Carriage and Insurance Paid

The seller pays for insurance as well as transport to the specified destination. Responsibility for the goods transfers to the buyer when the seller passes them to the first carrier.

Carriage and Insurance Paid is commonly used for goods being transported by container by more than one mode of transport. If transporting only by sea, CIF is often used (see above).

Chartered Insurance Professional

A professional designation granted by the Insurance Institute of Canada to insurance agents.

Commodity Import Program

A financing program of the United States government designed to expedite the payment for essential commodities to countries receiving United States economic aid. The program is administered by the Agency for International Development. The CIP

C

makes money available on a loan or grant for basic commodities and equipment (non-military, non-police, non-luxury products) that are needed by United States aid recipients. The commodities and products that are sent are exported from the United States and generally consist of such items as: foodstuffs, raw materials, chemicals, agricultural, transportation, and construction equipment, etc.

CIPD   Chartered Institute of Personnel and Development
(cipd.co.uk)

The world's largest Chartered HR and development professional body has an internationally recognised brand with over 135,000 members,

CIPFA   Chartered Institute of Public Finance Accountancy
(cipfa.org)

The professional body for people in public finance and the world's only professional accountancy body to specialise in public services

CIPS   Certified International Property Specialist

Professional certification from the National Association of Realtors.

CISI   Chartered Institute for Securities & Investment

A City of London-based professional body for those who work in the financial and investment industry.

CL   Capital Loss

Accounting and tax term for the occurrence of an investment being sold for less than the amount originally paid for it, sometimes with favorable tax consequences.

CLN   Construction Loan Note

Note issued by a municipality to finance construction of multi-family housing projects, generally maturing in three years or less and repaid with the proceeds of a long-term bond issue.

CLU   Chartered Life Underwriter
(www.theamericancollege.edu/insurance-education/clu-insurance-specialty)

Professional financial planning certification, most closely aligned with the life insurance industry.

CM   **Contribution Margin**

The difference between sales and the variable costs of the product/
service. The amount available to cover fixed costs and make
profits; also called *Marginal income*. For example:

Sales = $16,000

Variable costs = $8,000

Contribution Margin = $8,000 ($16,000 – $8,000)

CM (Variance)
Contribution Margin Variance

The difference between the actual contribution margin per unit
and the budgeted contribution margin times the number of units
sold. Thus:

- CM variance = (Actual CM per unit – Budgeted CM per unit)
  x Actual sales

- The greater the actual CM over the budgeted indicates a
  favorable condition.

CMA   **Certified Management Accountant**
(www.imanet.org/cma_certification.aspx)

The objectives of the CMA program are fourfold:

1. to establish management accounting as a recognized profession
   by identifying the role of the management accountant and
   financial manager, the underlying body of knowledge, and a
   course of study by which such knowledge is acquired;

2. to encourage higher educational standards in the management
   accounting field;

3. to establish an objective measure of an individual's knowledge
   and competence in the field of management accounting; and

4. to encourage continued professional development by
   management accountants.

Competitive Market Analysis

Real estate term for an analysis that uses information on generally
at least three sales of comparable properties in the recent past as
a tool to establish the fair market value, and therefore the listing
price for a property before placing it on the market.

CMBS **Commercial Mortgage-Backed Securities**

Securities backed by loans secured with commercial property, such
as retail businesses, office buildings, and multifamily homes.

C

CME **Chicago Mercantile Exchange**
(www.cmegroup.com)
Market that trades commodity futures and futures options.
Overall, the Chicago Board of Trade is probably bigger in number
of contracts traded per year, but the CME is bigger when it comes
to agricultural futures and "open interest" contracts.

CMFC **Chartered Mutual Fund Counselor**
(http://cffpdesignations.com/Designation/CMFC)
A new designation offered by the National Endowment for
Financial Education, showing a financial advisor's enhanced ability
to advise clients on their mutual fund questions and concerns.

CML **Council of Mortgage Lenders**
Is the trade association for the residential mortgage lending
industry in the UK.

CMO **Collateralized Mortgage Obligation**
Type of mortgage-backed bond that separates mortgage pools
into two maturity classes called tranches: companion bonds, and
planned amortization class bonds. CMOs generally give investors a
higher level of security than other mortgage-backed securities.

CMS **Cost Management System**
Cost and management accounting, control, and reporting system
that identifies, monitors, and maintains continuous, detailed
analyses of a company's activities and provides managers with
timely measures of operating results.

CMV **Current Market Value**
General business term for price at which willing buyers and sellers
trade similar products or services in an open marketplace.

CNS **Continuous Net Settlement**
Method of clearing and settling securities that eliminates multiple
fails in the same securities, accomplished by using a clearinghouse
and a depository to match transactions to securities available in
the firm's position, resulting in one net receive or delivery position
at the end of the trading day.

C

CNY **Chinese Yuan Renminbi**
The official currency of the People's Republic of China

COA **Chart of Accounts**

Accounting term for list of accounts for all types of income and expense, used as a tool for internal processing and reporting.

COBRA Congressional Omnibus Budget Reconciliation Act

Federal legislation that gives employees the right to carry their group health insurance coverage for up to 18 months after leaving the employer, by paying the full premium. The advantage to the employee is that the full premium of the group policy is generally lower than the individual rate on comparable coverage.

COBY **Current Operating Budget Year**

Accounting and general business term, usually identical to Fiscal Year.

COD **Cash on Delivery**

General business term for arrangement by which a freight or other delivery person receives payment in full from a customer in cash or certified check when delivery is made from a vendor. In securities, the requirement that delivery of securities to an institutional investor be in exchange for assets of equal value, which generally means cash; also *called delivery against cost* (DAC) or *delivery vs. payment* (DV).

CODA **Cash or Deferred Arrangement**

More commonly known as a 401(k) plan, an employee benefit plan in which employees can elect, as an alternative to receiving taxable compensation, to contribute part of their salary and other compensation pretax to a qualified tax-deferred retirement plan.

COFI **Cost-of-Funds Index**

Index based on what financial institutions are paying on money market accounts, passbooks, certificates of deposit and other liabilities, used by mortgage lenders to set rates on adjustable rate mortgages (*see* **ARM**). The COFI tends to move more slowly than other indexes for ARMs.

COLA **Cost of Living Adjustment**

General business term generally applied to salary and other pay-rate increases based on current national or local cost-of-living statistics.

C

COLI   **Cost of Living Index**

U.S. Government statistic, generally referred to as Consumer Price Index.

COLTS   **Continuously Offered Longer-Term Securities**

Investment banking term for category of securities.

COMPs   **Comparable Properties**

Properties similar to the subject property that are used to estimate the value of the subject property.

COO   **Chief Operating Officer**

Common job title for corporate officer responsible for day-to-day operations of the organization.

CPA   **Certified Public Accountant (USA)**

(www.aicpa.org)

Person holding an official certificate as an accountant, having fulfilled all legal and licensing requirements at the state level and with the AICPA.

CPA/PFS

Certified Public Accountant/Personal Financial Specialist
(www.aicpa.org/INTERESTAREAS/ PERSONALFINANCIALPLANNING)

Designation awarded by the American Institute of CPAs to CPAs who pass an exam and meet work experience requirements.

CPA Australia

Certified Practising Accountant Australia

(cpaaustralia.com.au)

An accounting body in Australia. Their core services to members include education, training, technical support and advocacy. Staff and members work together with local and international bodies to represent the views and concerns of the profession.

CPD   **Continuing Professional Development**

The means by which people maintain their knowledge and skills related to their professional lives.

CPI   **Consumer Price Index**

Often called the *cost-of-living index*. U.S. Government statistic reflecting the changes in the cost of buying a fixed bundle of goods (in the categories of food and beverages; housing; apparel; transportation; medical care; entertainment; and other) for a typical American family, based on the costs of the same goods and services at the base period established in 1967.

CPM   **Cost per Thousand**

An advertising term referring to the advertising costs of reaching 1,000 customers.

Critical Path Method

Project-management technique that uses a single time estimate for each activity, the primary objective being to identify the critical path for a project. *See also* **PERT**.

CPP   **Current Purchasing Power**

Accounting-measurement showing the effect of inflation on the value of money

CPSC   **Consumer Product Safety Commission**
(www.cpsc.gov)

The federal agency that deals specifically with the risks of injury resulting from a wide range of consumer products.

CPT   **Carriage Paid To**

The seller pays to transport the goods to the specified destination. Responsibility for the goods transfers to the buyer when the seller passes them to the first carrier.

CPU   **Central Processing Unit**

A component of a computer hardware system that combines control unit, storage unit, and arithmetic unit. The control unit interprets the instructions given to the computer. Internal storage is where the program of instructions is kept and where data from the input devices are sent. External storage can consist of disks and tapes. The arithmetic unit actually does the calculation required by the program. As technology advances, chip makers are finding ways to make the CPU smaller, faster, and more powerful.

C

CRAR **Capital to Risk Asset Ratio**

An analytical measure of bank capital adequacy and a tool for controlling bank risk.

CRAT **Charitable Remainder Annuity Trust**

A tax-exempt entity created as an estate-planning tool that pays a fixed and specified annuity amount to one or more person living at the inception of the arrangement, either for life or for a term of years not to exceed twenty.

CRB **Commodity Research Bureau Indexes**

The most widely followed commodity index. It is like the Dow Jones Industrial Averages (DJIA) for stocks. The index measures price changes in commodities, including soybeans, cocoa, coffee, sugar, cotton, and precious metals such as gold, platinum and silver. The Commodity Research Bureau (CRB) has two indexes: one is the CRB Spot Price Index and the other is the CRB Futures Price Index.

CRM **Customer Relationship Management**

A set of applications designed to gather and analyze information about customers. CRM systems automate customer service and support. They also provide for customer data analysis and support e-commerce storefronts. While CRM is constantly evolving, it's already led to some remarkable changes in the way companies interact with customers. The ultimate development of CRM remains to be seen but undoubtedly mobile communication will play a significant role. Many companies are already experimenting with systems to send messages to cell phone users offering them special discounts and buying "opportunities."

Example

Federal Express allows customers to track their packages on the Web. Amazon.com uses CRM technology to make suggestions to customers based on their personal purchase histories.

Cause-Related Marketing

A relatively narrow aspect of overall sponsorship which involves an amalgam of public relations, sales promotion, and corporate philanthropy. The distinctive feature of CRM is that a company's contribution to a designated cause is linked to customers' engaging in revenue-producing exchanges with the firm.

C

CRR **Cash Reserve Ratio**

A ratio of cash reserves or by way of current account with the Reserve Bank, computed to its demand and time liabilities. It aims at ensuring the safety and liquidity of the deposits with the banks.

CRT **Charitable Remainder Trust**

Accounting term for a planned giving vehicle in which an asset is placed in trust to benefit a charitable organization and the donor receives tax benefits.

CRUT **Charitable Remainder Unit Trust**

A tax-exempt entity that pays a fixed, specified percentage of the trust property valued annually to one or more person living at the inception of the arrangement, either for life or for a term of years not to exceed twenty.

CRV **Certificate of Reasonable Value**

Document from an appraiser or other valuation expert, describing an asset or piece of property and attesting to its value based on its current condition at a specific point in time.

C/S **Cost of Sale**

Accounting and general business term for expenses in connection with the sale of an asset.

CSP **Classification Settlement Program**

IRS program in which tax examiners can offer settlements to businesses that have incorrectly classified workers (*e.g.*, as independent contractors as opposed to full-time or part-time employees). The program is voluntary and businesses that decline an offered settlement retain their right to appeal.

CSR **Corporate Social Responsibility**

The concept that corporations can and should act ethically and be accountable to society for their actions, also known as *corporate social investment*.

CSVLI **Cash Surrender Value of Life Insurance**

Insurance term for the contract specified cash value of a life insurance policy if that option is exercised by the insured. The insurance premium consists of both expense and cash surrender value.

C

Example

A premium of $12,000 is paid that increases the cash surrender value by $8,000. The appropriate entry is:

Life Insurance Expense	4,000	
Cash Surrender Value of Life Insurance	8,000	
Cash		12,000

CTA   Cumulative Translation Adjustment Account

Account entry in a translated balance sheet where gains and/or losses from currency translation have accumulated over a period of years.

CTO   Chief Technology Officer

The head of the technology group. The CTO sorts through new ideas and products to identify those that are most relevant to the organization. The CTO's job requires deep knowledge of information technology and the ability to envision how various IT-related strategies will affect the organization over time. The title CTO is often viewed as synonymous with *Chief Information Officer*.

C2B   Consumer-to-Business E-Commerce

Online exchanges in which consumers search out sellers, learn about their offers, initiate purchases, and sometimes even driving transactions terms.

C2C   Consumer-to-Consumer E-Commerce

Web-based transactions between two consumers via the servers of a company, such as a auctions and sales. eBay is an example of a C2C site.

CTR   Currency Transaction Report

A report that federal law requires financial institutions to file 1. if they suspect criminal activity by a customer who is involved in a financial transaction of $1,000 or more or 2 when a single transaction of currency amounts to more than $10,000.

CVP   Cost Volume Profit

Useful for analyses by managers. It deals with how profit and costs change with a change in volume. Managers look at the relationships of costs, sales and net income to better cope with planning decisions and determine break-even sales (*i.e.*, the level of sales where total costs equal total revenue). A difference is made between variable and fixed costs in order to perform accurate CVP analysis. The following concepts are considered:

+CM (*Contribution Margin*) which is the excess of sales (S) over variable costs (VC) of a product. That is, it is the money available to cover fixed costs (FC) and produce profits. Thus,

CM = S –VC.

Unit CM, the excess of unit selling price (p) over the unit variable cost (v). Represented as

CM = p – v.

CM *Ratio* is the contribution margin as a percentage of sales. That is,

$$\text{CM ratio} = \frac{CM}{S} = \frac{S - VC}{S} = 1 - \frac{VC}{S}$$

CVP analysis determines what sales volume is needed to break even, volume needed to earn a desired profit, the profit expected on a given sales volume, how selling price, variable costs, fixed costs and output affect profit, and how changing the mix of products sold will affect break-even and income and profit potential.

Cost-volume-profit (analysis)

Deals with how profits and costs change with a change in volume.

CWO   Cash with Order

Merchandise is paid for when purchased rather than when delivered.

C

D

DA   Deposit Account

Accounting and banking term for an account that was established solely to receive deposited funds, from which funds are transferred to other accounts as necessary.

DAP   Delivered at Place

The seller pays for transport to the specified destination, but the buyer pays the cost of importing the goods. The seller takes responsibility for the goods until they're ready to be unloaded by the buyer.

DAT   Delivered at Terminal

The seller pays for transport to a specified terminal at the agreed destination. The buyer is responsible for the cost of importing the goods. The buyer takes responsibility until the goods are unloaded at the terminal.

DBA   Doing Business As

Certification by a state that a principal is doing business under an assumed name. The certificate also states the address where the business is being conducted. The primary purposes of the DBA certificate are:

1. registration of a business and its assumed name giving the principal's name and address.

2. protect the business name from being used by others.

3. provide a public source of redress.

DBMS   Data Base Management System

Group of computer software packages that integrates data in one place for sharing by all systems on a network, allowing cross-referencing of data among files to eliminate repetition.

DCA   Dollar Cost Averaging

A time diversified investment method in which a constant dollar amount of stock is bought at regularly scheduled dates. It is a constant dollar plan. This approach is especially appropriate for "blue chip" stocks. Because the same dollar amount of stock is invested in each period, less shares are purchased at higher prices and more shares are bought at lower prices. This strategy typically results in a lower average cost per share.

DCF   **Discounted Cash Flow**

1. Accounting and investment analysis concept that uses the future projected value of an investment discounted to its present-day value as a means of evaluating the relative merits of the investment. These techniques are used primarily for valuation.

2. Methods of selecting and ranking investment proposals such as the *net present value (NPV)* and *internal rate of return (IRR)* methods where time value of money is taken into account.

DDB   **Double-Declining Balance Depreciation Method**

Accounting and tax term for using an accelerated depreciation of certain types of assets in financial reporting and tax planning. It is the method that allocates the cost of an asset over its useful life based on a multiple of (often two times) the straight-Line rate

Example

An auto is purchased for $20,000 and has an expected salvage value of $2,000. The auto's estimated life is 8 years. Since the straight-line rate is 12.5 percent (1/8), the double-declining-balance rate is 25 percent (2 x 12.5%). The depreciation expense is computed as follows:

Year	Book Value at Beginning of Year	x	Rate (%)	=	Depreciation Expense	Year-end Book Value
1	$20,000		25		$5,000	$15,000
2	15,000		25		3,750	11,250
3	11,250		25		2,813	8,437
4	8,437		25		2,109	6,328
5	6,328		25		1,582	4,746
6	4,746		25		1,187	3,559
7	3,559		25		890	2,669
8	2,669		25		667	2,002

D

Note

If the original estimated salvage value had been $2,100 instead of $2,000, the depreciation expense for the eighth year would have been $569 ($2,669 – $2,100) rather than $667, since the asset cannot be depreciated below its salvage value.

DDP   **Delivered Duty Paid**

The seller is responsible for delivering the goods to the named destination in the buyer's country, including all costs involved.

DE   **Double Entry**

Accounting term for simultaneous entry of one transaction in two sets of records.

DENK   **Dual-Employed, No Kids**

Term for a category of taxpayers with common issues: married couples both of whom work, without children. (similar to **DINK**; *Also see* **DEWK**)

DEWK   **Dual-Employed, With Kids**

Term for a category of taxpayers with common issues: married couples both of whom work, with children. (*Also see* **DENK, INK**)

DF   **Degree of Freedom**

Number of data items that are independent of one another. Given a sample of data and the computation of some statistics (e.g., the mean), the degrees of freedom are defined as The number of observations included in the formula minus The number of parameters estimated using the data. For example, the mean statistic for N sample data points has n DF, but the variance formula has (n-1) DF because one parameter (the mean X) has to be estimated before the variance formula can be used.

DFL   **Degree of Financial Leverage**

Percentage change in earnings available to common shareholders that is associated with a given percentage change in net operating income. The greater the DFL, the riskier the firm; however, if the return on assets exceeds the cost of debt, additional leverage is favorable.

D

DIF   **Data Interchange Format (File)**

Computer system feature that allows for the transfer of files between systems and between different programs in the same system, such as between a spreadsheet program and a word-processing program.

DINK **Double Income, No Kids**

Term similar to **DENK**; *Also see* **DEWK**.

DISC **Domestic International Sales Corporation**

Domestic corporations created by the Revenue Act of 1971 to encourage exports and, thus, improve the balance of trade.

DJIA **Dow Jones Industrial Average**

Most widely followed stock market average, a benchmark stock average of 30 blue chip industrial stocks selected for total market value and broad public ownership and believed to reflect overall market activity, established in 1884.

DKK **Danish kroner**

The currency of Denmark, Greenland and the Faroe Islands,

DMS **Database Management System**

The software (computer programs) used to manage data in the database. It is a set of programs that provides for defining, controlling, and accessing the database. The database program allows managers to enter, manipulate, retrieve, display, select, sort, edit, and index data. Advantages of a database management system include: (1) elimination of data redundancy, (2) Improved efficiency in updating, (3) data sharing; (4) easy data access, and (5) reduced program maintenance cost. An example of database management systems is Microsoft Access.

DN **Debit Note**

Written promise to pay a specified amount to a named entity on demand or on a specified date.

DOA **Documents of Acceptance**

An international trade procedure used for payment of goods.

DOL **Degree of Operating Leverage**

Change in operating income (earnings before interest and taxes) resulting from a percentage change in revenues. It measures the extent to which a firm incurs fixed rather than variable costs in operations. Thus, the greater the DOL, the greater the risk of loss when sales decline, and the greater the reward when sales increase.

D/P   Deferred Payment

Accounting and general business term for arrangement in which payment for goods or services is not required at the time the goods or services are delivered.

DPI   Disposable Personal Income

Tax accounting and financial planning term for personal income not needed for basic necessities and therefore available for discretionary expenditures, such as travel, entertainment, etc.

DPO   Days Payable Outstanding

Accounts payable/(annual credit purchases/365). An estimate of the length of time the company takes to pay its vendors after receiving inventory. It is compared to company and industry averages, as well as company selling terms (e.g., Net 30) for determination of acceptability by the company.

DPP   Direct Profit Profitability

Accounting process that is capable of calculating net profitability of individual items of fast moving consumer goods.

DPS   Dividends per Share

The ratio showing how much the shareholders were actually paid by way of dividends. The formula: Dividends per share = Dividends paid to common shareholders/Average number of common shares.

DRIP   Dividend Reinvestment Plan

Investment vehicle (such as stock) in which dividends are automatically used to purchase additional shares rather than paid out to the investor.

DSO   Days of Sales Outstanding

Accounts receivable/(annual credit sales/365). A ratio that expresses how rapidly the firm is collecting its credit accounts. It is compared to company and industry averages, as well as company selling terms (e.g., Net 30) for determination of acceptability by the company.

DSS   **Decision Support System**

Computer software that supports decision-making processes, including planning and forecasting, risk and trend analysis and what-if analyses.

DT   **Debits Tax**

Australian taxation term.

DTB   **Deutsche Terminborse**

Fully computerized exchange in Germany

DTC   **Depository Trust Company**

Member of the Federal Reserve System owned by brokerage houses and the New York Stock Exchange, a centralized securities repository where stock and bond certificates are exchanged.

DTL   **Degree of Total Leverage**

Percentage change in net income that is associated with a given percentage change in sales. It is the product of the degree of financial leverage (dfl) and the degree of operating leverage (dol).

DUS   **Dollar Unit Sampling**

Auditing test that uses a probability proportionate to size sampling of audit units with a high precision level of possible error based on dollar mistakes found in a random sample, combined with an attribute resulting from a probability determination. DUS is generally used only when a low rate of sampling errors is expected.

DVA   **Discovery Value Accounting**

Australian accounting method.

D

E

EAFE   Europe, Australia, and Far East Index

Compiled by Morgan Stanley Capital International (MSCI), the Morgan Stanley Europe, Asia, and Far East Index is a value-weighted index of the equity performance of major foreign markets. The EAFE index (it is pronounced EE-feh.) is, in effect, a non-American world index of over 1,000 stocks. It is considered the key "rest-of-the-world" index for U.S. investors, much as the Dow Jones Industrial Average is for the American market. The index is used as a guide to see how U.S. shares fare against other markets around the globe. It also serves as a performance benchmark for international mutual funds that hold non-U.S. assets. Morgan Stanley also compiles indexes for most of the world's major stock markets as well as for many smaller, so-called "emerging" markets. In addition, there are Morgan Stanley indexes for each continent and the entire globe. The index is quoted two ways: one in local currencies and a second in the U.S. dollar.

EAN   Expenditure Account Number

Accounting term for general account used to paying day-to-day expenses of a business.

E&OE   Errors and Omissions Excepted

A British acronym. A legal disclaimer that notifies the reader that, without prejudice, that the content and/or validity of the subject data may change without notice.

EAPS   Employee Assistance and Wellness Programs

Programs designed to offer employees a variety of services that will help them to become mentally and physically healthy, which in turn reduces absenteeism and productivity losses due to accidents.

EBB   Economic Bulletin Board

A computer-based electronic bulletin board that provides leads and up-to-date statistical releases from the Bureau of Census, the Bureau of Economic Analysis, the Bureau of Labor Statistics, the Federal Reserve Board and other federal agencies.

EBIT   Earnings before Interest and Taxes

Accounting term used to clarify whether the accounting and reporting of an investment's earnings reflect interest and tax expenses.

EBITA   Earnings before Interest, Taxes, Depreciation and Amortization

Accounting term used to clarify whether the accounting and report of an investment's earnings reflect interest, taxes, etc.

EBITDA Earnings before Interest, Taxes, Depreciation, and Amortization

A type of pro forma computation used by financial analysts as a rough estimate of operating cash flows that are available to pay interest and other fixed charges.

EC   Electronic Commerce

The buying and selling of goods and services on the Internet, especially the World Wide Web. In practice, this term and a new term, "e-business," are often used interchangeably. For online retail selling, the term e-tailing is sometimes used. It is also called e-commerce for short, on-line commerce, Internet commerce, e-business, or cyberspace commerce. E-commerce can be divided into:

1. E-tailing or "virtual storefronts" on Web sites with online catalogs, sometimes gathered into a "virtual mall" It is the gathering and use of demographic data through Web contacts:

2. Electronic Data Interchange (EDI), the business-to-business exchange of data:

3. E-mail and fax and their use as media for reaching prospects and established customers (for example, with newsletters).

4. Business-to-business buying and selling.

5. The security of business transactions.

European Community

General business and economics term for specific group of European nations.

ECOA   Equal Credit Opportunity Act

A federal law making it illegal to discriminate when giving credit based on such factors as race, religion, marital status, and age. A lender must respond to credit applications within 30 days. If the application is denied, reasons must be given. The Federal Trade Commission is responsible for enforcing the provisions of the act.

ECU **European Currency Unit**

Composite currency created to function as a reserve currency numeraire. Consists of fixed amounts of the currencies of the members of the European Economic Community (EEC).

EDR **European Depository Receipt**

A means for trading of foreign investments by Americans in the securities of foreign countries.

EE **Equity Earnings**

Accounting and financial management term for earnings on investment equity.

EEC **European Economic Community**

General business and economics term for specific group of European nations.

EEO **Equal Employment Opportunity**

The government's attempt to ensure that all individuals have an equal chance for employment, regardless of race, color, religion, sex, age, disability, or national origin.

EERPF **Eastern European Real Property Foundation**

U.S. Government agency developed to educate Eastern European governments and executives about various aspects of the real estate industry and its practices in the U.S.

EFT **Electronic Funds Transfer**

Accounting and banking term for mechanism for automatic and paperless transfers of funds between accounts or organizations.

EFTPOS
Electronic Fund Transfer Point of Sale

An electronic payment which allows funds to be transferred from the account of the shopper to the merchant.

E

EFTPS **Electronic Federal Tax Payment System**

IRS system available to all taxpayers for filing tax returns and making tax payments electronically.

EGP **Egyptian Pound**

Is the currency of Egypt. It is divided into 100 piastres.

EIOP **End of Initial Operating Period**

Accounting and general business term for specific date established for end of a new enterprise's startup phase.

EIRIS **Ethical investment Research Service**

Is a global leader in the provision of environmental, social, governance (ESG) research for responsible investors.

EIS **Executive Information System**

System that provides information on how the company is currently performing in its operating and financial activities. The EIS provides detailed information as needed to bring management up-to-date in executive decision making.

EITF **Emerging Issues Task Force**

An entity formed in 1984 in response to the recommendations of the FASBs task force on timely financial reporting guidance and an FASB Invitation to Comment on those recommendations. Its mission is to assist the FASB in improving financial reporting through the timely identification, discussion, and resolution of financial accounting issues within the framework of existing authoritative literature.

EMP **End of Month Payment**

Accounting and banking term to indicate scheduled payment to/from a certain account.

EMQ **Economic Manufacturing Quantity**

Quantity a business or store should order to minimize the total inventory costs by minimizing inventory total cost that is being purchased against the best unit cost.

EMR **Experience Modification Rate**

Accounting and insurance term for the ratio of a company's losses to expected losses based on the industry and classification

E

averages over a three-year period. Used in calculating workers' compensation insurance premiums.

$$\frac{\text{Actual Losses}}{\text{Expected Losses}} = \text{EMR}$$

EMS European Monetary System

A small international monetary fund system formed in 1979 by 12 European countries. Under the system, member countries agreed to maintain their exchange rates within an established range about a fixed central rate in relation to one another.

EMTALA
Emergency Medical Treatment and Labor Act

The law, enacted by Congress in 1986, that requires emergency rooms to treat patients regardless of ability to pay. Patients must be admitted to the hospital or stabilized before they may be released.

EOM End of the Month

A credit designation that usually means payment is due at the end of the current month the purchase was made.

EOQ Economic Order Quantity

Model that determines the order size that minimizes the sum of carrying costs and order costs. At the EOQ amount, total ordering cost equals total carrying cost.

EOQ

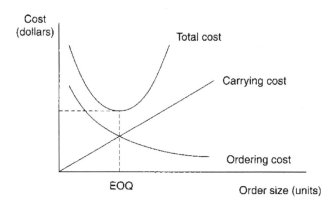

The EOQ is computed as:

$$EOQ = \sqrt{\frac{2D}{C}}$$

Example

Assume that the Buena Park Store buys sets of steel at $40 per set from an outside vendor. It will sell 6400 sets evenly throughout the year. The store desires a 16 percent return on its inventory investment, which is the interest charge on borrowed money. In addition, rent, taxes, etc., for each set in inventory is $1.60 per year. The ordering cost is $100 per order. Thus the carrying cost per set is 16%($40) + $1.60 = $8.00 per year. Therefore,

$$EOQ = \sqrt{\frac{2(6,400)(\$100)}{\$8.0}} = \sqrt{160,000} = 400 \text{ sets}$$

Number of times per year to place an order = $\frac{D}{EOQ}$ = $\frac{6,400}{400}$ = 16 orders

Total inventory costs = Carrying cost + Ordering cost

$$\frac{EOQ}{2} \times C + \frac{D}{EOQ} \times O$$

$$= \frac{400}{2} (\$8) + \frac{6,400}{400} (\$100)$$

$$= \$1,600 + \$1,600 = \$3,200$$

Based on these calculations, the Buena Park Store should order 400 sets of steel each time it places an order, and it should place an order 16 times during the year. This policy will be most economical, costing the store $3200 per year.

EOY   End of Year

Accounting term used in financial reporting to indicate financial information (actual or anticipated) for the end of the organization's fiscal year.

E

EPOS **Electronic Point of Sale**

A system that allows payments by debit or credit cards, and verifies transactions, provides sales reports.

EPR **Earnings Price Ratio (more commonly Price-Earnings Ratio)**

General financial term for ratio of a share's market price to the company's earnings per share.

EPS **Earnings per Share**

An accounting ratio comparing an entity's net income to its weighted average number of shares of common stock outstanding. This is the most widely watched ratio. EPS measures corporate operating performance and expected future dividends. The formula is:

$$EPS = \frac{\text{Net Income} - \text{Preferred Dividends}}{\text{Common Shares Outstanding}}$$

A decrease in EPS over the year should alert investor. This ratio must be disclosed on the face of the income statement. If the entity's capital structure is complex (i.e., having securities outstanding that could dilute earnings per share such as convertible preferred stock, convertible bonds, stock options, stock warrants) then a dual presentation of earnings per share must be disclosed on the face of the income statement including primary earnings per share and fully diluted earnings per share. In recent years, earnings per share has become one of the most important and well-known ratios in financial statement analysis.

ER **Expense Report**

General term for forms and other paperwork connected with accounting and reimbursement to individuals for certain business expenses (such as business travel and entertainment).

ERISA **Employee Retirement Income Security Act of 1974**

Federal legislation that enacted broad changes in retirement benefits for corporate employees.

ERM **Enterprise Risk Management**

A broad term for risk management system that

1. Makes each area manager responsible for documenting and evaluating financial controls in his or her own area. People

E

closest to each business unit manage the data, which improves accuracy and completeness.

2. Identifies areas with inadequate control measures so action plans can be initiated to resolve problems.

3. Tracks the progress of outstanding action plans, describes who is responsible for those actions, and sets the expected time for resolution.

4. Protects against fraud with systematic data management that ensures multiple reviews and verification.

5. Raises the level and precision of reporting to management.

6. Puts "localized knowledge" to work. Area managers become empowered to understand the impact of their roles on corporate results.

ERN   Eritrean Nakfa

Is the currency of Eritrea. It is divided into 100 cents.

ERP   Enterprise Resource Planning

A system that has the objective of providing an integrated system capability—a system that can run all the operations of a company and provide access to real-time data from the various functional areas of a entities objects about which data are produced and gathered.

ERTA   Economic Recovery Tax Act of 1981

Federal legislation that enacted broad changes to in general reduce income tax liabilities for U.S. taxpayers.

ES   Expert Systems

Computer software involving stored reasoning schemes and containing the knowledge of experts in an area. This is the area of Artificial Intelligence (AI) that has received great attention from business decision makers. There are recent advances in this area of software systems which are designed to mimic the way human experts make decisions. They represent an attempt to capture in computer program software the reasoning and decision making processes of human experts, providing computerized consultants. In effect, the expert system evaluates and solves problems requiring human imagination and intelligence that involve known and unknown information. The components of the systems include a knowledge base, inference engine, user interface, and knowledge acquisition facility.

ESOP **Employee Stock Ownership Plan**

Mechanism for converting all or part of the private ownership in a company into shares that are given to employees as bonuses, or sold to employees under certain terms.

ESS **Expert Support System**

Is a system that provides a full spectrum of services to help design, optimize and support an IT infrastructure.

ETF **Electronic Transfer Funds**

Equity indexes that were introduced in 1993 as a way for investors to buy into a liquid, transparent and diverse basket of stocks while paying less than for a mutual fund. The shares are priced in real time, tracking the value of their underlying index, and can be held as long-term investments, flipped for a quick profit or sold short to hedge equity risk.

Exchange Traded Funds

Mutual funds that change hands all day long on an exchange, just like stocks -- which is very different from the once-a-day trading of ordinary mutual funds.

EU **European Union**

The European Union is an economic and political union of over 28 member states that are in Europe.

EUP **Equivalent Unit of Production**

The concept used in *process costing*, that if 100 units are all 40% complete, then 40 whole units could have been completed.

EUR **Euro**

The official currency of the eurozone. It has symbol €.

EV **Economic Value**

Accounting and banking term for the monetary value of an asset, excluding intangible factors and possible future events that may affect the valuation.

EVA **Economic Value Added**

Variation of residual income (RI) that defines the variable in

E

specific ways. EVA = After-tax Income – (Cost of Capital x Capital Invested). The major difference between RI and EVA is that RI uses the market value or book value of assets for the capital invested in the division or firm while EVA uses the market value of total equity and interest-bearing debt. *See also* **RI.**

EVPI   Expected Value of Perfect Information

The difference between the expected value with perfect information and the expected value with current information. It is thus the maximum amount a decision maker would be willing to pay for additional information that gives a perfect indication as to the state of nature.

Eximbank
Export-Import Bank
(www.exim.gov)

The U.S. agency charged with providing the backbone support for American exports through credit risk protection and funding programs; also called as *EX-IM bank* for short throughout the world. The programs provided through the Export-import Bank of the United States make international factoring more feasible because they offer credit assurance alternatives that promise funding and sources the security they need to agree to a deal.

EXW   Ex Works

The seller makes the goods available to be collected at their premises and the buyer is responsible for all other risks, transportation costs, taxes and duties from that point onwards. This term is commonly used when quoting a price.

Example

Goods are being picked up by the seller from the buyer's premises in Hong Kong. The term used in the contract is EXW Hong Kong

E

FA   Fixed Asset

Accounting term for an asset whose value is generally not subject to fluctuations caused by market forces.

FAQ   Frequently Asked Questions

In the Internet and in many newsgroups, questions commonly asked by the users

FAS   Financial Accounting Standard

Declaration by the Financial Accounting Standards Board regarding the correct meaning and application of a particular financial accounting rule.

Free Alongside Ship

The seller puts the goods alongside the ship at the specified port they're going to be shipped from. The seller must get the goods ready for export, but the buyer is responsible for the cost and risk involved in loading them.

This term is commonly used for heavy-lift or bulk cargo (e.g. generators, boats), but not for goods transported in containers by more than one mode of transport (FCA is usually used for this).

FASAB   Federal Accounting Standards Advisory Board
(www.fasab.gov)

A U.S. federal advisory committee whose mission is to develop *generally accepted accounting principles (GAAP)* for federal financial reporting entities.

FASB   Financial Accounting Standards Board
(www.fasb.org)

An official independent rule- making body in financial accounting in the United States consisting of seven full-time members and a significant support staff. The FASB engages in research and issues authoritative pronouncements establishing GAAP in the form of FASB Statements and Interpretations.

It provides financial reporting and disclosure guidelines. The pronouncements must be adhered to by corporations and their outside auditors (CPA firms). It succeeded the AICPAs Accounting Principles Board. The issuances of the FASB are acceptable to the SEC and AICPA.
See also **SEC**; **GAAP**.

FBT   Fringe Benefits Tax

Any federal income tax paid on an employee benefit received outside of salary but classified by the IRS as taxable income to the employee.

FC   Full Charge

Accounting and general business term indicating that a cost will be charged and paid at 100% and not discounted.

FCA   Free Carrier

The seller gives the goods, cleared for export, to the buyer's carrier at a specified place. The seller is responsible for getting them to the specified place of delivery. This term is commonly used for containers travelling by more than one mode of transport.

The Financial Conduct Authority
(fca.org.uk)

Regulates the financial services industry in the UK. Their aim is to protect consumers, ensure the industry remains stable and promote healthy competition between financial services providers.

FCBA   Fair Credit Billing Act

A law designed to correct errors and abuses in credit billing and the handling of credit complaints. This act established time limits within which bills must be sent and complaints answered.

FCC   Federal Communication Commission

A government agency that regulates broadcast media and can eliminate ads that are deceptive or offensive.

FCIA   Foreign Credit Insurance Association

A private U.S. insurance carrier that insures exporters.

F

FCPA **Foreign Corrupt Practices Act**

A law designed to prevent U.S. companies from offering or giving bribes (directly or indirectly) to foreign officials for the purpose of influencing those officials (or causing them to use their influence) to help the companies obtain or retain business.

FCRA **Fair Credit Reporting Act**

Act that requires an employer to notify job candidates of its intent to check into their credit. This Act, enforced by the Federal Trade Commission, is designed to promote accuracy and ensure the privacy of the information used in consumer reports. Recent amendments to the Act expand your rights. Businesses that supply information about candidates also have new responsibilities under the law.

FDI **Foreign Direct Investment**

Investment that involves ownership of a company in a foreign country. In exchange for the ownership, the investing company usually transfers some of its financial, managerial, technical, trademark, and other resources to the foreign country. It is distinguished from foreign portfolio investment.

FDIC **Federal Deposit Insurance Corporation**

The federal agency that insures bank accounts. Most commercial and all national bank accounts carry FDIC insurance up to $100,000. It is important to note that insurance is for each depositor and not for each account. If the amount held by one depositor exceeds $100,000, another account should be opened with a different bank, or additional deposits with the same bank could be made in another person's name.

FET **Federal Estate Tax**

Area of the federal tax code concerned with taxpayers' estates and those parts that are transferred to others or passed on to heirs.

Federal Excise Tax

Taxes on certain consumer items, such as alcohol, tobacco, gasoline, firearms and airline tickets.

FFB **Federal Financing Bank**
(www.treasury.gov/ffb)

U.S. government corporation, created by Congress in 1973

under the general supervision of the Secretary of the Treasury. The FFB was established to centralize and reduce the cost of federal borrowing, as well as federally-assisted borrowing from the public. The FFB was also established to deal with federal budget management issues which occurred when off-budget financing flooded the government securities market with offers of a variety of government-backed securities that were competing with Treasury securities. Today the FFB has statutory authority to purchase any obligation issued, sold, or guaranteed by a federal agency to ensure that fully guaranteed obligations are financed efficiently.

FFO   **Funds from Operations**

A term used in real estate and real estate investment trusts (**REITs**) to present the cash flow from trust operations i.e., earnings plus depreciation and amortization.

FGI   **Finished Goods Inventory**

That portion of goods in inventory which have completed and are available for sale.

FGL   **Financial General Ledger**

Accounting term interchangeable with General Ledger.

FGT   **Federal Gift Tax**

Area of the federal tax code concerned with taxpayers' gifts to others and the tax benefits and liabilities thereby created.

FHA   **Federal Housing Administration**

U.S. Government agency that provides mortgage insurance on loans made by FHA-approved lenders throughout the United States and its territories. FHA insures mortgages on single family and multifamily homes including manufactured homes and hospitals. It is the largest insurer of mortgages in the world, insuring over 34 million properties since its inception in 1934.

FHFA   **Federal Housing Finance Agency**
(www.fhfa.gov)

U.S. Government agency that oversee vital components of our country's secondary mortgage markets – Fannie Mae, Freddie Mac, and the Federal Home Loan Banks. It was created on July 30, 2008 as a result of the Housing and Economic Recovery Act of 2008.

F

FHLMC Federal Home Loan Mortgage Corporation
(www.freddiemac.com)
Commonly called Freddie Mac, also refers to mortgage-backed
securities packaged, guaranteed and sold by the organization.

FIA   Fixed Income Account
Accounting and banking term for account of a fixed-income
investment.

FIC   Financial Inventory Control
Accounting term for practices connected with monitoring
inventory, ordering levels, and inventory costs.

**FICA   Federal Insurance Contributions Act, commonly known as
Social Security**
Federal legislation that provides retirement income and health
benefits to the elderly, disabled and other qualifying individuals
and families.

FICO   Fair, Isaac & Company Credit Score.
A computer-generated credit score that predicts a lender's risk in
doing business with a borrower. Any company or individual that
issues mortgage loans, home-equity loans, car loans, insurance
policies, or healthcare services (even the IRS) bases much of its
lending decisions and terms on the applicant's FICO score. FICO
scores are determined by computers and released through the
three credit bureaus to their subscribing members. At Experian.
the scores are called *Experian/Fair, Isaac*; at Equifax, they are called
Beacon scores; at Trans Union, they are called *Empirica* scores.
FICO scores five main kinds of credit information. Listed from
most important to least important showing the percentage of the
score based on the category, the categories are: Payment history
(approximately 35% of the score), amount owed (approximately
30% of the score), length of credit history (approximately 15%),
new credit (approximately 10%), and types of credit in use
(approximately 10%). Credit scores range from 300 to 850. Scores
provide an extremely valuable guide to future risk based solely on
credit report data. The higher the consumer's score, the lower the
risk to lenders when extending new credit to a consumer.

FICR   Financial Inventory Control Report
Accounting and business management term for periodic reporting

of inventory levels and costs used to optimize use of financial resources.

FICS   Financial Information Control System

Accounting and business management term for systems governing flow, management and access to financial information.

Forecasting and Inventory Control System

Accounting and business management term for system that anticipates and plans for inventory fluctuations.

FIFO   First In, First Out

A method of inventory costing based on the assumption that the costs of merchandise sold should be charged against revenue in the order in which the costs were incurred.

Example

Assume the following data regarding inventory during the year.

	Units	Unit Cost	Total Cost
Beginning Inventory, October 1	1,000	$5.00	$5,000
Purchases:			
October 3	3,500	6.00	21,000
October 9	4,000	7.00	28,000
October 19	2,000	8.00	16,000
October 25	2,000	9.00	18,000
Total	12,500	$88,000	
Number of units in cost of goods available for sale			12,500
Number of units sold			10,000
Number of units in ending inventory			2,500

Under FIFO, the year-end inventory valuation and the cost of goods sold are:

F

October 19	500	$8.00	$4,000
October 25	2,000	9.00	18,000
Total	2,500		$22,000
Cost of goods available for sale			$88,000
Less: Ending inventory			22,000
Cost of goods sold			$66,000

See also **LIFO**.

FIR   Financial Inventory Report

Accounting and business management term for periodic inventory report.

FIRREA Financial Institutions Reform, Recovery and Enforcement Act

Federal tax legislation enacted in 1989 to resolve the crisis in the savings and loan industry.

FIS   Fiscal Information System

Accounting and business management term for general financial management information systems.

FISH   First In, Still Here

Facetious accounting term for unsold, aging inventory. *Also see* **FIFO, FIST, LIFO**.

FIST   First In, Still There

Facetious inventory accounting term. *Also see* **FIFO, FISH, LIFO**.

FIT   Federal Income Tax

Broad area of the federal tax code concerned with tax obligations owed on all types of income (earned income, capital gains, etc.)

FITW   Federal Income Tax Withholding

Accounting and tax term for systems of withholding Federal Income Taxes from payments to workers for payment directly to the U.S. Government.

F

FIVE C'S

Five C's Credit

Five elements used by lenders in evaluating a borrower's credit application. They are:

1. Character (willingness to pay)
2. Capacity (cash flow)
3. Capital (wealth)
4. Collateral (security)
5. Conditions (economic conditions)

Character reflects a customer's integrity and reliability in meeting financial obligations. The borrower's credit history indicates how reliable the borrower is in paying bills on time. Capacity looks at a borrower's earning power and/or cash flow. Capital analyzes a borrower's balance sheet (assets and liabilities revealing whether net worth is positive or negative). Collateral refers to assets that can be secured and liquidated by the lender if a loan is not repaid. Finally, conditions mean economic conditions at the time of the loan and a borrower's vulnerability to business downturn or credit crunch. When much money is available, especially at low interest rates, it is much easier to obtain credit, whereas in a credit crunch, many applicants would be rejected who would normally have been approved for credit. Once the five C's are analyzed, a borrower is assigned to a credit rating category, which will determine the default risk premium for the borrower. Generally, the higher a customer's credit risk, the higher the loan rate.

5W2H   5 Whys, 2 Hows Approach

Asking various questions about the current process and how it can be improved. 5W2H refers to "why, when, who, where, what, how to do, and how not to do."

FJA   Functional Job Analysis

Quantitative approach to job analysis that utilizes a compiled inventory of the various functions or work activities that can make up any job and that assumes that each job involves three broad worker functions: (1) data, (2) people, and (3) things.

FLR   Fixed Loan Rate

Accounting and banking term for fixed lending rate as opposed to variable rate over the life of a loan.

F

FLSA **Fair Labor Standards Act**

Act enacted in 1938 that applies to workers involved in interstate commerce. It sets standards with respect to working condition, including such aspects as minimum wage and working hours. It has been periodically amended and adjusted to keep the standards relevant to the current working environment.

FMLA **Family and Medical Leave Act**

The law that requires governmental employers and the private employers of 50 or more workers to provide their employees up to 12 weeks of unpaid leave for their own serious illness, the birth or adoption of a child, or the care of a seriously ill child, spouse, or parent.

FMR **Fair Market Rent**

Business and real estate term for the rental rate based on comparisons to rental rates to similar properties in similar locations at same period of time.

FMRR **Financial Management Rate of Return**

Accounting and real estate investment term for analysis that measures return on investment during length of ownership, refined to remove certain distortions during periods of negative cash flow. *Also see* **IRR**.

FMS **Flexible Manufacturing System**

Computer-controlled process technology suitable for producing a moderate variety of products in moderate, flexible volumes. This system reduces setup or changeover times and facilitates the production of differentiated products in small numbers. The shift in emphasis is from mass production of a few products to a job-shop environment in which customized orders are manufactured. Automation allows for better quality and scheduling, rapid changes in product lines, and lower inventories and costs. *See also* **CIM**.

FMV **Fair Market Value**

1. Amount that could be received on the sale of a security in the market. There exist willing and financially capable buyers and sellers who have informed knowledge; also called market value. No unusual circumstances exist such as emergencies.

2. Appraisal amount derived by an independent appraiser.

F

3. In real estate, tax, and other applications, the market value, or the value someone is willing to pay. Current value of a property.

FNMA Federal National Mortgage Association
(www.fanniemae.com)

U.S. government-sponsored enterprise that was created in 1938 to expand the flow of mortgage money by creating a secondary mortgage market. Fannie Mae is a publicly traded company which operates under a congressional charter that directs Fannie Mae to channel its efforts into increasing the availability and affordability of homeownership for low-, moderate-, and middle-income Americans.

FOB   Free On Board

Under the Incoterm standard published by the International Chamber of Commerce, FOB stands for "Free On Board", and is always used in conjunction with a port of loading. Indicating "FOB *port*" means that the seller pays for transportation of the goods to the port of shipment, plus loading costs.

FOK   Fill or Kill

In securities brokerage, signifies a buy or sell order that will be cancelled if a complete transaction is not executed.

FOMC Federal Open-Market Committee
(www.federalreserve.gov/fomc)

Division of the Federal Reserve Bank, responsible for setting interest rates and credit policies for the Federal Reserve System. Economists and market analysts watch the Committee's decisions closely as a means of predicting action by the Fed to stimulate the economy by tightening or loosening credit.

FOREX Foreign Exchange

The exchanges of the currency of one country for that of another country. Foreign exchange (FOREX) is not simply currency printed by a foreign country's central bank. Rather, it includes such items as cash, checks (or drafts), wire transfers, telephone transfers, and even contracts to sell or buy currency in the future. Foreign exchange is really any financial that fulfills payment from one currency to another. The most common form of foreign exchange in transactions between companies is the *draft* (denominated in a foreign currency). The most common form of foreign exchange in transactions between banks is the telephone

F

transfer. Foreign Exchange is the backbone of all international capital transactions. The FOREX market has vital implications for the economic prospects of the countries concerned and the general prosperity of the free world economy. The reason is that some $1.5 trillion worth of international currencies are bought and sold every single trading day. *(www.knewmoney.com)*. This volume of trade is equivalent to over two months of trading in the New York Stock Exchange. *Note:* A foreign exchange market is now available to individual investors for trading foreign exchanges.

4/5th Rule
4/5th Rule

The rule stating that discrimination generally is considered to occur if the selection rate for a protected group is less than 80% of the group's representation in the relevant labor market or less than 80% of the selection rate for the majority group.

four Is   **four Is (of services)**

Four basic characteristics that distinguish services from goods: intangibility, inseparability of production and consumption, inventory, and inconsistency. These characteristics are important because they pose several unique marketing problems.

FOUR Ps
Four Ps

Four basic elements in the *marketing mix – product, place, price, and promotion.*

FP   **Fully Paid**

Accounting and bookkeeping term for an invoice or loan paid in full.

FRB   **Federal Reserve Board**
(www.federalreserve.gov)

Governing board of the USA Federal Reserve System, establishing Federal Reserve System policies on reserve requirements and other bank regulations, setting the discount rate, controlling the availability of credit in the country, and regulating the purchase of securities on margin.

FRC   **Financial Reporting Council**

The UK's independent regulator responsible for promoting high quality corporate governance.

F

FREIT **Finite Life Real Estate Investment Trust**

A Real Estate Investment Trust (*see* **REIT**) that is established with the goal of selling its holdings within a specified period of time to realize capital gains.

FRN **Floating Rate Note**

A short-term debt obligation where the interest rate is variable. It is linked to a market rate such as the 3-month T-bill rate or London Interbank Offer Rate (**LIBOR**).

FRS **Financial Reporting Standard**
(frc.org.uk)

Sets the framework of codes and standards for the accounting, auditing, in the UK.

FSA **Financial Services Authority**
(www.fsa.gov.uk)

Formerly the UK's leading financial regulator charged with maintaining market confidence, promoting public understanding of the financial system, protecting customers and combating financial crime.

The FSA has now become two separate regulatory authorities The Financial Conduct Authority (**FCA**) and The Prudential Regulation Authority (**PRA**)

Financial Statement Analysis

An approach used by investors, managers, suppliers, and lenders to appraise the past, current, and projected financial condition and performance of a company. Ratio analysis is the most important type of financial analysis. It provides relative measures of a company's financial condition and operating performance. Horizontal analysis is used to evaluate the trend in the accounts over the years. Vertical analysis (common size analysis) looks at the relationship of an account to a total with the same year such as cost of sales or item sales. It discloses the internal structure of the entity. Vertical analysis reveals the relationship between sales and each income statement account. It represents the mix of assets that generate income and the mix of debt and equity financing. When using financial ratios, comparisons should be made of a company's ratios over the years to identify trends. In determining relative performance, comparisons should also be made between a company's ratios and industry norms (averages), as well as

F

a company's ratios to competing companies in the industry.
Examples of financial ratios are summarized below.

Ratios	Definitions
Liquidity	
Net working capital	Current assets – current liabilities
Current Ratio	Current assets/current liabilities
Quick (Acid-test) ratio	(Cash + marketable securities + accounts receivable)/current liabilities
Cash Ratio	Cash/current liabilities
Cash burn rate	Current assets/average daily operating expenses
Asset Utilization	
Accounts receivable turnover	Net credit sales/average accounts receivable
Average collection period	365 days/accounts receivable turnover
Inventory turnover	Cost of goods sold/average inventory
Average age of inventory	365 days/inventory turnover
Operating cycle	Average collection period + average age of inventory
Cash conversion cycle	Operating cycle – average payable period
Total asset turnover	Net sales/average total assets
Solvency	
Debt ratio	Total liabilities/total assets
Debt-equity ratio	Total liabilities/stockholders' equity
Times interest earned	Income before interest and taxes/ interest expense
Cash coverage Ratio	EBITD/interest
Free cash flow (FCF)	Cash flow from operations - cash used to purchase fixed assets - cash dividends

F

Ratios	Definitions
Profitability	
Gross profit margin	Gross profit/net sales
Profit margin	Net income/net sales
Return on total assets (ROA)	Net income/average total assets
Return on equity (ROE)	Earnings available to common stockholders/average stockholders' equity
Market Value	
Earnings per share (EPS)	(Net income -preferred dividend)/ common shares outstanding
Price/earnings (P/E) ratio	Market price per share/EPS
Book value per share	(Total stockholders' equity – preferred stock)/common shares outstanding
Price/book value ratio	Market price per share/book value per share
Market value added (MVA)	market value of the firm's stock – equity capital supplied by shareholders
Dividend yield	Dividends per share/market price per share
Dividend payout	Dividends per share/EPS

Flexible Spending Account

A tax-advantaged financial account that can be set up through a cafeteria plan of an employer in the United States

FSC Foreign Sales Corporation

Established by the Tax Reform Act of 1984. The FSC is a foreign corporation that exports for a United States firm. The firm may show its profits in the FSC and avoid U.S. taxation on a percentage of the earnings until they are remitted to the parent U.S. firm.

FTC Federal Trade Commission

(www.ftc.gov)

U.S. Government agency charged with investigating and enjoining illegal practices in interstate trade.

F

FTI **Federal Tax Included**

Accounting term to indicate that federal taxes are included in a certain number.

Foreign Traders Index

The index, compiled by the United States and Foreign Commercial Service, covers information about foreign entities, including addresses, contact persons, revenue, company size, and product or services offered.

FTP **File Transfer Protocol**

Protocol associated with the transfer of information on the Internet between client computers and file servers. Files may be transferred, downloaded, and uploaded individually or in batch form.

FTT **Federal Transfer Tax**

Large area of the federal tax code that comprises three tax regimes: federal estate tax (FET); federal gift tax (FGT); and the generation-skipping tax (GST).

FUTA **Federal Unemployment Tax Act**

Federal and state legislation that requires employers to contribute to a fund that pays unemployment insurance benefits for employees.

FV **Face Value**

Australian accounting and banking term for the value of a bond, note or security as given on the certificate or instrument.

Future Value

Accounting and financial analysis term for projected value of an investment at a specified point in time.

FVIF **Future Value Interest Factor**

Projected value of an investment of $1 at a specified point in time. It is found in Table 1 (T1) in the Appendix.

FVIFA **Future Value Interest Factor of an Annuity**

Projected value of an investment of an annuity of $1 at a specified point in time. It is found in Table 2 (T2) in the Appendix.

F

FVO   **For Valuation Only**

Related to *FYI*—For Your Information.

FY   **Fiscal Year**

Accounting term for a business entity's financial reporting year (*e.g.*, January 1 through December 31, or July 1 through June 30)

FYDS   **Fiscal Year Data Summary**

Accounting term for a preliminary or interim financial report.

FYE   **Fiscal Year Ending**

Accounting abbreviation, such as "FYE 30 June 2013."

FYM   **Fiscal Year Month**

Accounting term used when the numbers 1 through 12 rather than months' names are used in financial reporting and recordkeeping, such as "FYM1" in place of January.

FYO   **Fiscal Year Option**

Accounting term for an entity's opportunity to change its financial reporting year, for instance from January 1 through December 31, to July 1 through June 30, to accommodate certain seasonalities in business cycles.

F

G

G   Gigabyte

A multiple of the unit byte for digital information storage. A billion or so bytes.

G&A   General and Administrative Expenses

The costs incurred for administrative activities (e.g., executive salaries and legal expenses). It is simply called administrative expenses.

GAAP   Generally Accepted Accounting Principles

Standards, conventions, guidelines, rules and procedures accountants follow in recording and summarizing transactions, and in the preparation of financial statements. GAAP is based on authoritative accounting pronouncements, such as American Institute of CPAs' Opinions, Financial Accounting Standards Board Statements, industry practice, and accounting literature in the form of books and articles. In the audit report, the CPA must indicate that the client has followed GAAP on a consistent basis.

GAAS   Generally Accepted Auditing Standards

The general rules and guidelines that an auditor must follow in fulfilling his professional responsibilities in the audit of an entity's financial statements. GAAS includes considerations of the auditor's professional qualities such as technical training, independence and competence as well as standards of reporting and fieldwork. The broadest guidelines that auditors must follow in the performance of an audit are the ten generally accepted auditing standards (GAAS) that were developed by the American Institute Of Certified Public Accountants (AICPA) in 1947 and have remained fundamentally the same over the years. The most authoritative guidance currently available to auditors are the Statement on Auditing Standards (SAS) issued by the Auditing Standards Board of the AICPA. SASs are viewed as interpretations of the ten GAAS previously noted. Together, GAAS and SAS represent the current collective authoritative guidance that auditors must follow in the performance of an audit.

GAI   **General Accounting Instructions**

Accounting term for internal documents codifying day-to-day and other accounting and financial management and reporting practices and requirements.

GAO   **General Accounting Office**
(www.gao.gov)

A legislative branch, headed by the Comptroller General, that was established to assist the Congress in its oversight of the executive branch and to serve as the independent legislative auditor of the Federal Government. Among others, roles of the GAO are: (1) prescribing principles and standards for Federal agency accounting systems; (2) assisting agencies in accounting system design; and (3) reporting to Congress on the status of agency accounting systems.

GARP   **The Global Association of Risk Professionals**

The only globally recognized leader in financial risk testing and certification programs, and educational and training activities.

GAS   **General Accounting Service**

British agency similar to U.S. Financial Accounting Standards Board.

GASB   **Governmental Accounting Standards Board**
(www.gasb.org)

U.S. Government agency establishing accounting standards for both government and business.

GATR   **Gross Average Tax Rate**

Australian tax term.

GATT   **General Agreement on Tariffs and Trade**

An agreement signed at the Geneva Conference in 1947 which became effective on January 1, 1948. It set a framework of rules and guidelines for international trade, including a negotiation of lower international trade barriers, and settling trade disputes. Over the years, the agreement has been modified, as needed, through various rounds of negotiations. GATT also acts as an international arbitrator with respect to trade agreement abrogation. More specifically, GATT has four basic long-run objectives: (1)

G

reduction of tariffs by negotiation, (2) elimination of import quotas (with some exceptions), (3) nondiscrimination in trade through adherence to unconditional most-favored-nation treatment, and (4) resolution of differences through arbitration and consultation.

GBP   United Kingdom Pound

Currency of the UK with a symbol £

GCM   General Counsel Memoranda

Background documents that the IRS uses to support a ruling, useful to accountants as research tools to interpret the Internal Revenue Code (IRC).

GD   Gross Debt

Accounting business term for total loans outstanding to creditors.

GDP   Gross Domestic Product

An economic indicator that measures the value of all goods and services produced by the economy within its boundaries and is the nation's broadest gauge of economic health. GDP is divided among personal consumption, investment, net exports, and government spending. Consumption makes up roughly two-thirds of the total. GDP is normally stated in annual terms, though data are compiled and released quarterly. The U.S. Bureau of Economic Analysis releases an advance estimate of quarterly GDP, followed by a "preliminary" estimate and a "final" figure. It is reported as a "real" figure, that is, economic growth minus the impact of inflation. The figure is tabulated on a quarterly basis, coming out in the month after a quarter has ended. It is then revised at least twice, with those revisions being reported once in each of the months following the original release. Changes in the GDP of the U.S. are calculated quarterly, and announced in annualized terms (what the annual change would be if the quarter's pace of growth or contraction continued for a year). GDP reports appear in most daily newspapers and online at services like America Online. Also visit the Federal Government Statistics Web site on the Internet at *www.bea.gov/bea/newsrel/gdpnewsrelease.htm, www.fedstats.gov/* or *www.economicindicators.gov*. GDP is often a measure of the state of the economy. For example, many economists speak of recessions when there has been a decline in GDP for two consecutive quarters. The GDP in dollars and real terms is a useful economic indicator.

G

GE   **Gross Earnings**

Accounting term for an entity's total earnings (e.g., both dividends and interest) in a given earnings period.

G-8   **Group of Eight**

A forum for governments of eight nations of the northern hemisphere: Canada, France, Germany, Italy, Japan, Russia, the United Kingdom, and the United States; in addition, the European Union is represented within the G8. The 2009 G-8 Summit, held in June 2009 in Italy came to an end with the approval of seven joint declarations on the issues of the economic crisis, poverty, climate change and international political issues.

GEM   **Growing Equity Mortgage or Growth Equity Mortgage**

Fixed-rate home loan with a fixed interest rate for the life of the loan, but annual payment increases as set by the loan agreement, with the increases applied directly to the principal. This type of loan is often attractive to first-time homebuyers and others who cannot afford a large down payment or higher interest payments during the early years of the loan, but whose earning power can be expected to increase over the life of the loan.

GI   **Gross Income**

1. The amount of money earned (which is collected or will be collected) from the sale of goods minus the cost of the goods sold, also called gross profit or gross margin. For example, assume sales is $4,000 and the cost of goods sold is $1,200, the gross income is $2,800 ($4,000 - $2,800). Gross profit less operation expenses equals net income.

2. To the IRS, gross income is gross taxable income, salary, any investment earnings, and any other income subject to income tax.

GIC   **Guaranteed Investment Contract**

Contract between an insurance company and a corporation's profit sharing or pension plan that guarantees a specific rate of return on invested capital over the life of the contract.

GIGO   **Garbage In – Garbage Out**

Inputting incorrect data in computers which leads to inaccurate results.

G

GIM   **Gross Income Multiplier**

A method of determining the price to pay for an income-producing property by dividing the asking price (or market value) of the property by the current gross rental income.

Example

Assume that current gross rental income = $23,600 and the asking price = $219,000, then the gross income multiplier is $219,000/$23,600 = 9.28.

A property in the similar neighborhood may be valued at "8 times annual gross." Thus, if its annual gross rental income amounts to $23,600, the value would be taken as $188,800 (8 x $23,600). This approach should be used with caution. Different properties have different operating expenses which must be taken into account in determining the value of a property.

GJ   **General Journal**

Accounting term for day-to-day bookkeeping records of receipts and disbursements.

GL   **General Ledger**

Accounting term for bookkeeping of all financial records.

GLA   **General Ledger Account**

Accounting and bookkeeping term for account active within an entity's general ledger system.

GLAC   **General Ledger Account Code**

Accounting term for an account used at all levels of the general ledger system for consistency.

GLAPPAR
General Ledger, Accounts Payable, and Accounts Receivable

Accounting term for this group of accounting and bookkeeping functions.

GLIC   **General Ledger Identification Code**

Accounting term for coding of items for consistency.

GLSA   **General Ledger Subsidiary Account**

Accounting term for secondary level of general ledger bookkeeping.

GMAT   Graduate Management Admission Test

Is a computer adaptive test (CAT) which assesses a person's skills in standard written English in preparation for being admitted into a graduate management program.

GMV   Guaranteed Minimum Value

General business and marketing term for a value below that a commodity is guaranteed by the vendor not to fall.

GNMA   Government National Mortgage Association
(www.ginniemae.gov)

Commonly called Ginnie Mae, a government-owned corporation that primarily issues securities that pass through all payments of interest and principal received on a pool of federally insured mortgage loans. GNMA guarantees that all payments of principal and interest will be made on the mortgages on a timely basis.

GNP   Gross National Product

The monetary value of all the goods and services, minus depreciation and consumption, produced in a country.

GPM   Graduated Payment Mortgage

Real estate lending instrument in which payments gradually increase over a set period and the interest rate is adjusted periodically according to a specified economic index.

GPP   General Purchasing Power

Economics term for aggregate potential for consumption among a specific demographic population.

GRAT   Grantor Retained Annuity Trust

An estate-planning mechanism in which an asset is placed in a trust for a certain period of time and the grantor receives income from an annuity. If the donor dies before the term expires, then the entire value of the transferred property, valued at the donor's death, is taxed as part of the donor's gross estate for federal estate tax (FET) purposes. However, if the donor survives the term, the entire property is passed to the donee at only a fraction of the federal gift tax (FGT) value that would otherwise attend such passing.

G

GRIT **Grantor Retained Income Trust**

Financial planning vehicle for passing increased wealth to heirs by reducing estate and inheritance taxes, and protecting the grantor's primary residence from the claims of creditors.

GRM **Gross Rent Multiplier**

The ratio of the selling price of property to its gross rental income. It is a popular income method that is used to appraise an income producing property. For example, if the selling price of property was $350,000 and the gross rental income generated was $50,000, the GRM would be 7 times.

GSI **Gross Scheduled Income**

Real estate income as derived by multiplying monthly rent per current lease by 12 months.

GST **Generation-Skipping Tax**

Large area of the federal tax code concerned with gifts and exemptions available to all taxpayers against transfers during life or at death, and the estate-planning mechanisms that can be used to create long-term trusts that protect assets from over-taxation.

GTC **Good Till Cancelled**

A customer's order to a broker to buy or sell securities at a specified price, which is to remain in effect until it is either executed, or cancelled by the customer.

G-20 **Group of Twenty**

An informal forum that promotes open and constructive discussion between industrial and emerging-market countries on key issues related to global economic stability. By contributing to the strengthening of the international financial architecture and providing opportunities for dialogue on national policies, international co-operation, and international financial institutions, the G-20 helps to support growth and development across the globe. The Group of Twenty (G-20) Finance Ministers and Central Bank Governors was established in 1999 to bring together systemically important industrialized and developing economies to discuss key issues in the global economy. The inaugural meeting of the G-20 took place in Berlin, on December 1516, 1999, hosted by German and Canadian finance ministers.

G

GUI   **Graphical User Interface**

A program interface that takes advantage of the computer's graphics capabilities to make the program easier to use. It uses the easy-to-use icons and pull-down windows which give a program its commands.

GULP   **Group Universal Life Policy**

Life insurance policy offered to employees and, sometimes, their family members, on a group basis, therefore less expensively than individuals could obtain personally.

G

H

HA   House Account

Financial management. An account handled at the main office of a brokerage firm or managed by an executive of the firm, as distinguished from an account managed by a salesperson.

HC   Hard Copy

Business management term for a physical paper document as opposed to an electronic document.

Holding Company

Business management term for a corporation that owns enough voting stock in another corporation to influence its board of directors and therefore to control its policies and management.

HEL   Home Equity Loan

Loan that uses the borrower's primary residence and equity as collateral, generally used to finance home improvements, generally with financing terms more attractive than the borrower would be able to obtain with a conventional loan.

HIC   Highly Indebted Country

International finance term for nations carrying large amounts of indebtedness to other nations.

HICB   Hong Kong Industrial and Commercial Bank

HKD   Hong Kong Dollar

Currency of Hong Kong

HK$ Hong Kong Dollar alternative

HKFE   Hong Kong Futures Exchange

HKFE merged with the Stock Exchange of Hong Kong, and together with Hong Kong Securities Clearing Company formed Hong Kong Exchanges and Clearing Limited.

HKMEx Hong Kong Mercantile Exchange

In 2013 the exchange ceased to trade upon surrendering its authorisation to provide automated trading services

HLT   Highly Leveraged Transaction

Loan, usually by a bank to a company whose capital structure includes debt in addition to equity .

HMO   Health Maintenance Organization

Relatively recent development in health-care plans for employees of businesses and others in which individuals' needs are served by certain providers as opposed to individually chosen physicians, etc., to control costs and set and maintain certain standards of care.

HMRC   Her Majesty's Revenue and Customs (HMRC)

Is a non-ministerial department of the UK Government responsible for the collection of taxes

HP   Half Pay

Business management term for a 50% rate reduction in a worker's fee for a given period for a specific reason.

Half Price

Business management for a 50% price discount on a product or service.

HPI   House price index

A broad measure of the movement of single-family house prices, calculated by Federal Housing Finance Agency (www.fhfa. gov). The HPI is a weighted, repeat-sales index, meaning that it measures average price changes in repeat sales or refinancings on the same properties. This information is obtained by reviewing repeat mortgage transactions on single-family properties whose mortgages have been purchased or securitized by Fannie Mae or Freddie Mac since January 1975.

HPR   Holding Period Return, or annual rate of return

The total return earned from holding an investment for the holding period of time.

HPR for mutual funds is calculated by incorporating dividends, capital gains and price appreciation being ending NAV – beginning NAV. The formula is:

$$HPR = \frac{[\text{Dividend} + \text{Capital gain distribution} + (\text{Ending NAV} - \text{Beginning NAV})}{\text{Beginning NAV}}$$

HRA   Human Resource Accounting

Specialized field within accounting dealing with human resources, payroll and employee benefits, taxes and other issues, generally viewing employees as valuable assets and striving to enhance the positive relationship between a business' success and the quality of its employees. Primary objectives include quantifying the business' human resources for use in decision-making, and evaluating and managing costs of turnover.

HRM   Human Resource Management

The part of the organization that is concerned with the "people" dimension. It involves staffing, training, management development, motivation, performance evaluation, compensation activities, and maintenance of employees so as to achieve organizational goals. HRM is complicated in an international business by the profound differences between countries in labor markets, culture, legal systems, economic systems, and so on.

HR-10   Keogh Pension Plan

A tax-deferred retirement plan established by a Self-Employment Individual Tax Retirement Act of 1962 (HR-10) under which self-employed persons have the right to establish for themselves and their employees retirement plans that permit them the same tax advantages available to corporate employees covered by qualified pension plans; also known as *HR-10 plan*. The contributions are tax deductible, and earnings are tax deferred until withdrawn. Keogh plans can take different forms, such as a defined benefit plan, a defined contribution plan, or a hybrid plan.

HTML   Hypertext Markup Language

Uniform coding for defining Web documents. The browser used by the user examines the HTML to ascertain the manner in which to display the graphics, text, and other multimedia components. The use of HTML is recommended in developing intranets/extranets because it is easier to program than window environments such as Motif or Microsoft Windows. HTML is a good integrating tool for database applications and information systems. It facilitates the use of hyperlinks and search engines enabling the easy sharing of identical information among different responsibility segments of the company. Intranet data usually goes from back-end sources (e.g., mainframe host) to the Web server to users (e.g., customers) in HTML format.

HTTP **Hypertext Transport Protocol**

The basic protocol for the World Wide Web (WWW).

HUD **U.S. Department of Housing and Urban Development** *(www.hud.gov)*

U.S. Government agency responsible for stimulating and guiding the housing development industry.

HZ **Hertz**

The frequency of electrical cycles per second. One Hz is equal to one cycle per second.

I

IA   **Inactive Account**

Banking and brokerage term for an account not generally used continually in a productive way.

IAAO   **International Association of Assessing Officers**

Chicago, Ill.-based trade organization of individuals offering a range of valuation and assessment services to business and industry.

IABK   **International Association of BookKeepers**

British-based trade organization.

IAFP   **International Association for Financial Planning**

Atlanta, Ga.-based trade organization.

IAHA   **International Association of Hospitality Accountants**

Washington, D.C.-based organization.

IAP   **Insurance Accounting Principles**

Accounting term for body of principles specific to insurance issues.

IAPC   **International Auditing Practices Committee**

A committee of the International Federation of Accountants (IFA) set up with the responsibility and authority to issue exposure drafts and guidelines on Generally Accepted Auditing Standards and the content and form of audit reports. The IAPC attempts, through the issuance of such guidelines, to establish uniformity in auditing standards throughout the world. As a committee of the IFA, the IAPC attempts to meet the goals of the IFA whose primary objective is the "development and enhancement of a coordinated worldwide accountancy profession with harmonized standards."

IAPM   **International Asset Pricing Model**

The international version of the CAPM in which investors in each country share the same consumption basket and purchasing power parity holds.

IAPS **International Auditing Practice Statement**

Report by auditors on compliance with international financial reporting standards.

IAR **Inventory Adjustment Rate**

Accounting term for rate applied to inventory under certain conditions to correct or clarify probable errors.

IARFP **International Association of Registered Financial Planners**

New Jersey-based trade organization.

IAS **International Accounting Standards**

A set of international accounting and reporting standards, developed and published by the International Accounting Standards Committee (IASC) from 1973 to 2000. Unless specific standards have been revoked, they are still valid in full today. Since the reworking of IAS 1 in 2003, the "old" IAS have been collectively referred to as IFRS. Any existing standards are developed further as IAS and all new standards are known as IFRS. This will help to harmonize company financial information, improve the transparency of accounting and ensure that investors receive more accurate and consistent reports.

IASB **International Accounting Standards Board**
(www.ifrs.org/Home.htm)

An independent regulatory body, based in the United Kingdom, which aims to develop a single set of global accounting standards.

IASC **International Accounting Standards Committee**
(www.iasc.org.uk)

A group which consists of members from influential accounting bodies in the United States, England, West Germany, France, Canada, Japan, etc. The organization proposes internationally accepted accounting standards. Discussion papers, drafts, and formal statements are issued. There is adherence to universally adopted and accepted concepts. It was founded in 1973.

IAU International Accounting Unit

The unit of measure used in NATO projects which is based on the exchange rates of the member nations and is reevaluated every six months.

IBAN   International Bank Account Number

Is an internationally agreed means of identifying bank accounts across national borders with a reduced risk of propagating transcription errors.

IBF   International Banking Facility

A banking operation within United States bank that allows it to accept euro currency deposits from foreign residents without the need for domestic reserve requirements, interest rates ceilings, or deposit insurance premiums.

IBNR   Incurred but Not Reported

Often used in reference to insurance claims, It is the estimated payout for services and products that haven't been taken into account at the time of a given financial report.

IBRD   International Bank for Reconstruction and Development (http://web.worldbank.org)

Also known as the World Bank, the organization that provides financing for commercial and infrastructure projects, mostly in developing nations.

IC   Incremental Cost

Accounting term for a cost factor that increases in proportion to one or more variables.

Independent Contractor

Business management term for an individual providing services or works for hire for a fee to a company as opposed to being an employee, in a relationship governed by IRS regulations and guidelines.

Investment Credit

See ITC - Investment Tax Credit.

Intellectual capital

The amount by which the market value of a firm exceeds its tangible (physical and financial) assets less liabilities.

ICA   International Congress of Accountants

An organization of the major professional organization of

accountants from countries across the globe whose purpose it is to deal with the problems associated with diversity of accounting principles and practice from country to country. The first major conference of the ICA was held in St. Louis in 1904 to discuss and exchange accounting information relating to the diversity of accounting practice from county to country. However, no real effort was made to establish accounting principle uniformity at this conference. At the Tenth International Congress of Accountants, held in Sydney Australia (1972), two new organizations were established to deal more effectively with the problem of accounting principle divergence. These two new organizations were the International Accounting Standards Committee (IASC) and the International Federation of Accountants both of which are in existence today. The primary goal of both of these groups is the development and enhancement of a worldwide harmonized set of accounting standards.

ICA A   Institute of Chartered Accountants Australia
(charteredaccountants.com.au)

Is the professional body for Chartered Accountants in Australia and members operating throughout the world.

IC&C   Invoice Cost and Charges

Accounting and bookkeeping term for the total amount of an itemized bill for goods or services as prepared by the seller, including the goods and services, and applicable taxes, delivery and other charges.

ICAEW   Institute of Chartered Accountants in England and Wales
(www.icaew.com)

National organization of Chartered Accountants in Britain and Wales. The Chartered Accountant (CA) license designation in England is equivalent to the Certified Public Accountant (CPA) license designation in the United States. The Institute of Chartered Accountants in England, like its American counterpart, the American Institute of Certified Public Accountants in the US, supports research and professional projects and publishes the monthly prestigious journal, Accountancy, for its readership. Topics commonly covered in the journal include: all areas of accounting, information systems, professional ethics, law, and general management.

ICC   Interstate Commerce Commission

A world business organization that promotes international trade, investment and the market economy system worldwide; makes rules that govern the conduct of business across borders; provides essential services, foremost among them the ICC International Court of Arbitration, the world's leading institution of its kind. Members from 63 national committees and over 7000 member companies and associations from over 130 countries throughout the world present ICC views to their governments and coordinate with their membership to address the concerns of the business community.

International Currency Codes

The International Organization for Standardization publishes a list of standard currency codes referred to as the ISO 4217 code list

International Chamber of Commerce

Is an international organization with its headquarters in France. It has three main activities: rule setting, arbitration and policy. Because its member companies and associations are themselves engaged in international business, ICC has unrivalled authority in making rules that govern the conduct of business across borders.

ICCA   Institut Canadien de Comptables Agrees
(www.icca.ca)

Canadian Institute of Chartered Accountants (CA). Its mission is to foster public confidence in the CA profession by acting in the public interest and helping our members excel

ICEM   Incremental Cost Effectiveness Model

Business management term for analytical framework for determining cost effectiveness of various possible outcomes given certain variables.

ICF   Investing Cash Flow

Cash flow statement that reports the aggregate change in a business's cash position as a result from any gains (or losses) from investments

ICFA   Institute of Chartered Financial Analysts
(www.cfainstitute.org)

An educational branch of the Financial Analysts Federation

which was founded in 1947. The ICFA grants the Chartered Financial Analyst (CFA) designation to persons who have met certain professional qualifications. Essentially, candidates must serve a 2-year apprenticeship and also pass a series of three annual examinations about such topics as accounting, economics, ethical standards and laws, and security analysis to obtain the CFA designation. The ICFA is headquartered at the University of Virginia, Charlottesville, Virginia.

ICFP **Institute of Certified Financial Planners**
(www.cfp.net)

Denver, Colorado-based organization that awards CFP® certification. The mission of Certified Financial Planner Board is to benefit the public by granting the CFP® certification and upholding it as the recognized standard of excellence for competent and ethical personal financial planning

ICGN **International Corporate Governance Network**
(www.icgn.org)

Founded in 1995, a formal network of investors, companies, academics, and finance experts created to provide a forum for communicating ideas regarding the development of global corporate governance practices.

ICM **Inventory Control Management or Inventory Control Manager**

Business management term for the function or job title associated with managing and valuing supplies, finished goods, etc., of a business.

ICOFR **Internal Control over Financial Reporting**

A process designed and maintained by management to provide reasonable assurance regarding the reliability of financial reporting and the preparation of the financial statements for external purposes in accordance with United States GAAP.

ICP **Inventory Control Point**

Accounting and business management term for a predetermined inventory level that triggers a certain event (*e.g.*, reordering) when reached.

ICR **Inventory Change Report**

Accounting and business management term for documentation completed to reflect an adjustment to inventory reporting, either as a correction or to record goods received, etc.

ICS **Issued Capital Stock**

Brokerage term for stock sold by a corporation or entity at a particular time.

ID **Interest Deductible**

Tax accounting term for loan interest that is deductible against corporate or individual income tax.

Issue Date

Brokerage term for date on which stock or securities were available for purchase.

IDB **Industrial Development Bond**

Type of municipal revenue bond issued to finance fixed assets that are then leased to private firms, whose payments amortize the debt.

IDEA **Interactive Data Electronic Application**

A system that replaces Edgar. IDEA is a different approach than EDGAR. IDEA provides investors with easier and quicker access to financial information about public companies. IDEA uses data-tagging software akin to bar codes for financial data. The technology is based on the extensible business reporting language (XBRL). It allows for fast comparisons of different business entities or different time periods. The information will be available at no cost searchable on the Internet.

IDR **Industrial Development Revenue Bond**

Interchangeable with Industrial Development Bond (IDB).

Invoice Discrepancy Report

Accounting and business management term for a periodic report summarizing variances between departments or functions in terms of amount invoiced and amount received.

IEA   International Energy Agency

(www.iea.org)

An autonomous agency linked with the Organization for Economic Cooperation and Development (OECD). It is the authoritative source for energy statistics worldwide and an energy policy advisor for 26 member countries. It was founded during the oil crisis of 1973-74 and was initially focused on coordinating efforts between member countries in times of oil supply emergencies. Since then it has expanded its role to encompass climate change policies, market reform, energy technology collaboration, and outreach to the rest of the world.

IET   Interest Equalization Tax

Tax of 15% on interest received by foreign borrowers in U.S. capital markets, imposed in 1963 and discontinued in 1974.

IF   Insufficient Funds

Accounting and banking term applied to a bank draft written on an account that lacks adequate funds to pay the amount of the draft.

IFAC   International Federation of Accountants

(www.ifac.org)

The global organization for the accountancy profession. It works with its 164 members and associates in 125 countries and jurisdictions to protect the public interest by encouraging high quality practices by the world's accountants. IFAC members and associates, which are primarily national professional accountancy bodies, represent 2.5 million accountants employed in public practice, industry and commerce, government, and academia.

IFRS   International Financial Reporting Standards

Standards and interpretations adopted by the International Accounting Standards Board (IASB). Many of the standards forming part of IFRS are known by the older name of International Accounting Standards (IAS). IFRS are sometimes confused with IAS, which are the older standards that IFRS replaced. IAS was issued from 1973 to 2000. The implementation in 2005 of IFRS as the reporting language for all listed companies in the European Union and for many others around the world has been one of the biggest revolutions in the accounting world for a generation. The Financial Accounting Standards Board (FASB) and International Accounting Standards Board (IASB) are committed to crafting one set of accounting standards. The goal of the convergence project is to unify accounting standards, which in turn should improve comparability of financial statements across national jurisdictions.

IFS   Institute of Fiscal Studies

A UK based organization whose aim is to promote effective economic and social policies by understanding better their impact on individuals, families.

ifs School of Finance
The ifs School of Finance

A not-for-profit professional body and registered charity incorporated by Royal Charter. The only specialist provider of professional financial education that is able to award its own taught degrees.

IIA   Institute of Internal Auditors
(www.theiia.org)

A professional organization that was established to develop the professional status of internal auditing. It administers and confers the CIA (Certified Internal Auditor). *See also* **Certified Internal Auditor (CIA)**.

ILC, ILOC
Irrevocable Letter of Credit

Instrument or document issued by a bank guaranteeing the payment of a customer's drafts up to a stated amount for a specified period and which cannot be cancelled.

ILCCTC International Liaison Committee on Co-operative Thrift and Credit

Paris, France-based international finance organization.

ILO   International Labor Office
(www.ilo.org)

An affiliate of the United Nations composed of unions, employers, and governments dealing with trade union rights, employment terms and conditions, and the protection of the right to work and organize and bargain collectively.

ILS **Israeli Shekel**

Official currency of Israel

I/M **Inventory Management**

Business management term for the functions involved with managing materials, works in progress, supplies used in operations, and finished goods.

IMA **Institute of Management Accountants**

(www.imanet.org)

The association for accountants and financial professionals

The worldwide association for accountants and financial professionals working in business, representing more than 60000 members. It awards the CMA certificate.

IMF **International Monetary Fund**

(www.imf.org)

A fund created at the Bretton Woods agreement in 1944 to supervise the international financial system, to lend official reserves to nations with temporary payments deficits, and to decide when exchange rate adjustments are needed to correct chronic payments deficits. The IMF has an international paper currency called *special drawing rights (SDRs)* to increase international liquidity. The IMF is affiliated with the United Nations and funded by member contributions.

Inventory Master File

Business management document or record, physical or electronic, that compiles all materials and items in inventory.

IMIS **International Management Information System**

A computer-based or manual system which gathers, stores, processes, disseminates, and transforms data into information useful in the support of decision making in international business environments. Data come from the two main sources: (1) Internal sources: market analysis, special reports, data from Macs' sales, accounting, manufacturing, financial records as reported by foreign subsidiaries or affiliates, agents, representatives, and customers. (2) External sources: Reports and financial statistics from central and commercial banks, multinational trade organizations, trade associations, international business and finance periodicals, industry representatives, and home and host countries.

IMM   **International Monetary Market**

Division of the Chicago Mercantile Exchange (Merc) that trades futures in U.S. Treasury bills, foreign currencies, certificates of deposit and Eurodollar deposits. IMM publishes the IMM *Weekly Report*. The *Report* covers interest rate markets, gold and selected cash market information such as the prime rate and the federal funds.

International Money Management

Financial policies used by multinational companies aiming at optimizing profitability from currency and interest rate fluctuation while controlling risk exposure.

IMS   **Inventory Management System**

Business management term for systems and procedures, physical and electronic, involved with day-to-day management of the business' inventory, directed at maximizing profits by creating a strong balance between investment in inventory and smooth, continuous production.

IN   **Interest**

Cost of using money expressed as a rate per period of time.

Incoterms
   Incoterms

Rules or International Commercial Terms are a series of pre-defined commercial terms published by the *International Chamber of Commerce*

INR   **Indian Rupee**

Official currency of India

IO   **Interest Only**

Banking term for a type of loan in which the only current obligation is interest and repayment of the principal is deferred.

IOD   **Institute of Directors**

A worldwide association of members with headquarters in London, the Institute of Directors provides a professional network for all corners of the business community.

I

IOP **Initial Operating Period**

Business management term for time period (generally one year) considered a new business' startup period and in which financial performance needs to be viewed differently.

IOS **International Organization for Standardization**

Publishes a list of standard currency codes referred to as the ISO 4217 code list.

IOU **I Owe You**

Written acknowledgement of a debt, especially an informal one, generally consisting only of the sum owed and the names and signatures of the parties involved

IP **Installment Paid**

Accounting and Bookkeeping term to indicate that a specific installment on a long-term loan has been paid in full.

Insolvency Practitioners

In the United Kingdom, only an authorised or licensed Insolvency Practitioner (usually abbreviated to IP) may be appointed in relation to formal insolvency procedures.

IPA **Insolvency Practitioners Association**

A membership body recognised for the purposes of authorising (licensing) insolvency practitioners (IPs)

IPE **International Petroleum Exchange**

London-based energy futures and options exchange.

IPO **Initial Public Offering**

A corporation's first offering of stock to the public. It is typically an opportunity for the present investors, participating venture capitalists, and entrepreneurs to make big profits, since for the first time their shares will be given a market value reflecting expectations for the company's future growth.

IPRS **Intellectual Property Rights**

The ownership of the right to possess or otherwise use or dispose of products created by human ingenuity. Examples are trademarks, patents, trade names, trade secrets and copyrights. There are international organizations, which deal solely with intellectual property, such as *International and Territorial Operations.*

IR   Investor Relations

Internal function of an investment organization that is responsible for producing communication materials for the firm's clients and various publics.

IRA   Individual Retirement Account

A personal, tax-deferred retirement account that an employed person can set up with deposits and their earnings tax-deferred under certain tax regulations.

IRB   Industrial Revenue Bond

Interchangeable with Industrial Development Bond (IDB) and Industrial Development Revenue Bond (IDR).

IRC   Internal Revenue Code

Term for the group of statutes and regulations comprising the federal tax law of the U.S.

IREF   International Real Estate Federation
(www.fiabci.org)

Paris-based organization offering programs and services for individuals and organizations involved or interested in international real estate investment.

IREM   Institute of Real Estate Management
(www.irem.org)

Chicago-based organization offering programs, products and services for property managers of all types of real estate, offers the Accredited Residential Manager (ARM) and Certified Property Manager (CPM) professional designations and publishes the *Journal of Property Management* (JPM).

IRP   Interest Rate Parity

A state where the difference between national interest rates for securities of similar risk and maturity should be equal to but opposite in sign to the forward exchange rate differential between two currencies. The premium (P)/discount (D) are calculated as follows:

I

$$P \text{ (or D)} = \frac{-r_f - r_d}{1 + r_f}$$

where rf and rd equal foreign and domestic interest rates.

IRPEG   Imposta sull Reddito delle Persone Giuridiche

Tax on legal entities. An Italian taxation term.

IRR   Internal Rate of Return

Discount rate at which the present value (PV) of the future cash flows of an investment equals the cost of the investment (I); also called *time adjusted rate of return*. That is, at IRR, I=PV, or NPV (net present value) = 0. Under the internal rate of return method, the decision rule is: accept the project if IRR exceeds the cost of capital; otherwise, reject the proposal.

Example

Consider the following data:

Initial investment $12,950

Estimated life 10 years

Annual cash inflows $ 3,000

Cost of capital (minimum required return) 12%

We will set up the following equality (I=PV):

$12,950 = $3,000 x T4

Then T4 = $12,950/$3,000 = 4.317, which stands somewhere between 18% and 20% in the 10-year line of Table 4 in the Appendix.

Note

Excel has a function IRR(*values, guess*). Excel considers negative numbers as cash outflows such as the initial investment, and positive numbers as cash inflows. Many financial calculators have similar features. Suppose you want to calculate the IRR of a $12,950 investment (the value "-12950" entered in year 0, followed by 10 monthly cash inflows of $3,000). Using a guess of 12% (the value of 0.12), which is in effect the cost of capital, your formula would be @IRR(values, 0.12) and Excel would return 19.15%, as shown below.

Year 0	1	2	3	4	5	6	7	8	9	10
–12950	3000	3000	3000	3000	3000	3000	3000	3000	3000	3000

IRR = 19.15%

IRRC **Investor Responsibility Research Center**
(www.irrcinstitute.org)

Founded in 1972, an independent company that provides research on corporate governance and social responsibility issues for institutional investors.

IRS **Interest Rate Swap**

A contractual arrangement between two parties who agree to exchange interest payments on a defined principal amount for a fixed period of time.

Internal Revenue Service
(www.irs.gov)

U.S. Government agency charged with collecting most federal taxes, administering U.S. Department of Treasury regulations, and investigating and resolving tax illegalities.

IRSC **Internal Revenue Service Center**

Any of a number of regional centers throughout the U.S. responsible for processing federal tax returns and refunds, and which serve as regional headquarters for IRS auditors and investigators.

IS **Income Statement**

Interchangeable with Profit and Loss (P&L) Statement, a summary of revenues, costs and expenses of a company during an accounting period.

I/S **Inventory to Sales Ratio**

Ratio that shows how many times the inventory of a business is sold during an accounting period.

ISA **International Standard on Auditing**

Professional standards for the performance of financial audit of financial information.

ISCEBS **International Society of Certified Employee Benefit Specialists**
(www.iscebs.org)

The interactive community providing educational resources,

innovative thinking and collective wisdom to help members excel and prosper in their careers. This membership organization is for those who have earned the Certified Employee Benefit Specialist (CEBS), Group Benefits Associate (GBA), Retirement Plans Associate (RPA) and Compensation Management Specialist (CMS) designations

ISE   International Stock Exchange of the United Kingdom (U.K.) and the Republic of Ireland

Organization that replaced the London Stock Exchange after its merger with the International Securities Regulatory Organization.

ISM   Institute for Supply Management's index

The index, based on a survey of 375 companies in 17 industries, which measure new orders, inventories, exports, and employment in the service sector. Services account for five-sixths of the $10-trillion U.S. economy and include industries such as entertainment, utilities, health care, farming, insurance, retail, restaurants and zoos.

ISO   Incentive Stock Option

Plan under which qualifying options are free of tax at the date of grant and the date of exercise, and profits on shares sold are subject to capital gains taxes depending on the length of time the shares are held.

International Organization for Standardization
(www.iso.org)

A worldwide federation of national standardization bodies of more than 140 countries. Established as a non-government organization in 1947, it develops international standards and publishes them. All branches other than electrical engineering standards are within the scope of ISO.

ISO 9000
International Organization for Standardization 9000

ISO 9000 certification standards developed by the International Organization for Standardization (ISO) that serves as a basis for quality standards for global manufacturers. The 9000 is a block of numbers set aside for manufacturing standards, whereas other block numbers are for other standards.

ISP   **Internet Service Provider**

Business to service customers so they may access the Internet (such as America Online), and sometimes other related services, to subscribers.

IT   **Income Tax**

Annual tax on personal and corporate income levied by the government and by certain local governments.

ITA   **International Trade Administration**
(http://trade.gov)

Previously known as the United States Tariff Commission, the United States Trade Act of 1974 augmented the organization's responsibilities to regulate and protect American trading interests and insure that all of the country's trading activities are in accordance with US law and treaties. A primary function of the International Trade Administration is to oversee imports, import duties, and assess the effect of the foreign imports structure on the United States economy. Some other responsibilities of the ITA includes: determining the necessity of import duty relief for domestic industries, providing counsel concerning trade negotiations, investigating unfairly traded, subsidized, or dumped manufactured or agricultural imports entering the country, monitoring the trading activities of America's trading partners, etc.

International Trade Association
(www.ita.doc.gov)

A division of the United States Dept. of Commerce who offers to help United States exporters and businesses compete in the global marketplace. It has information about export opportunities for specific industries, as well as information about specific nations.

ITC   **Investment Tax Credit**

Reduction in income tax liability granted by the federal government to firms making new investment in certain asset categories; also called Investment Credit (IC).

International Trade Commission
(www.usitc.gov)

An independent, nonpartisan, quasi-judicial federal agency that provides trade expertise to both the legislative and executive branches of government, determines the impact of imports on

U.S. industries, and directs actions against certain unfair trade practices, such as patent, trademark, and copyright infringement.

ITF   **In Trust For**

Financial management designation for assets held through a fiduciary relationship by one individual (trustee) for another (beneficiary).

IT/R   **Inventory Transfer Receipt**

Bookkeeping term for documentation involved in transferring inventory from one location or account to another.

ITS   **Intermarket Trading System**

Video/computer display system that links the posts of specialists at the New York, American, Boston, Midwest, Philadelphia and Pacific Stock Exchanges and NASD market makers who trade the same securities. A transaction that is accepted by a broker at one exchange is analogous to an "electronic handshake" and constitutes a contract.

IV   **Improved Value**

Real estate term for a stated value of a property that includes both land and existing improvements (structures) thereon.

IVA   **Inventory Valuation Adjustment**

Accounting and bookkeeping term for a revision to the valuation of one or more inventory items.

IWP   **Internal Working Paper**

Accounting term for general notes and worksheets maintained as reference and background to an accounting project and generally not included in the final documents.

J

JA   **Joint Account**

Financial management and banking term for a bank or brokerage account that is owned jointly by two or more people.

JAS   **Job Accounting System**

Accounting and systems management term for a computer system designed to compile and monitor costs and expense items on a project-by-project basis.

JIT   **Just In Time**

Business management term for inventory management and purchasing system whereby materials are ordered on an as-needed basis to minimize storage and other costs and to ensure that product is as up-to-date as possible. It is a business philosophy that focuses on eliminating time, cost, and poor quality within manufacturing processes. JIT is a demand-pull system. Demand for customer output (not plans for using input resources) triggers production. Production activities are "pulled", not "pushed," into action. The major differences between JIT manufacturing and traditional manufacturing are summarized below.

Comparison of JIT and Traditional Manufacturing

JIT	Traditional
1. Pull system	1. Push system
2. Insignificant or zero inventories	2. Significant inventories
3. Manufacturing cells	3. "Process" structure
4. Multifunction labor	4. Specialized labor
5. Total quality control (TQC)	5. Acceptable quality level (AQL)
6. Decentralized services	6. Centralized services
7. Complex cost accounting	7. Simple cost accounting

J

JO   **Job Order**

Business management term for the documentation generated internally or between a customer and a supplier or vendor to establish the specifications and costs of a job or order.

Joint Ownership

In business management, equal ownership by two or more people, who generally have right of survivorship.

JOA   **Joint Operating Agreement**

In business management, a contract between two individuals or entities for the terms of shared operation of property or an enterprise or venture.

JPY   **Japanese Yen**

Official currency of Japan.

JSE   **Johannesburg Stock Exchange**

The largest stock exchange in Africa.

JY   **Japanese Yen**

Official currency of Japan

J

K

KCBT   **Kansas City Board of Trade**

An American commodity futures and options exchange regulated by the Commodity Futures Trading Commission.

KD   **Knocked Down**

Business management term for unassembled materials or merchandise.

KWD   **Kuwaiti Dinar**

Currency of Kuwait

KYD   **Cayman Islands Dollar**

Currency of the Cayman Islands

L

LA   **Leasehold Area**

Real estate term for a detailed description and specifications of property in which a lessee or tenant has a lease, including how the leased area was measured.

Ledger Account

Accounting and bookkeeping term for account book(s) or records of final entry.

Liquid Asset

Asset or property that can be quickly converted into cash.

LAIS   **Loan Accounting Information System**

In accounting and systems management, a computer system designed to compile and monitor costs and expense items on a loan-by-loan basis.

LAN   **Local Area Network**

Generally, a collection of microcomputers and peripherals, such as hard disk drives and laser printers, linked together by connections that provide cost-effective sharing of data and hardware among all linked users who are usually all located in the same building. There are three basic LAN configurations:

1. Star, in which a central host computer has a number of microcomputers wired to the host.
2. Ring, in which multiple computers are connected through a continuous communications cable without a central computer.
3. Bus or Tree, in which a series of microcomputers or peripherals are connected to a central cable and to which other computers or peripherals can be added by tapping into the central cable.

LAWN   **Local Area Wireless Network**

A LAN connected by radio rather than actual wires.

LBO   **Leveraged Buyout**

Business management and finance term for the takeover of a

company using borrowed funds, then repaying the debt from the company's assets.

LC; L/C Letter of Credit

Instrument or document issued by a bank guaranteeing the payment of a customer's drafts up to a stated amount for a specified time period. There are three primary L/Cs used in international trade that can be irrevocable or revocable and are summarized in the following table:

	Irrevocable confirmed L/C	Irrevocable unconfirmed L/C	Revocable L/C
Who applies for	Importer	Importer	Importer
Who is obligated to pay	Issuing bank and confirming bank	Issuing bank	None
Who applies for amendment	Importer	Importer	Importer
Who approves amendment	Issuing bank, exporter, and confirming bank	Issuing bank and exporter	Issuing bank
Who reimburses paying bank	Issuing bank	Issuing bank	Issuing bank
Who reimburses issuing bank	Importer	Importer	Importer

There are also other types of letter of credit:

- *Letter of credit (Cumulative)* – A revolving letter of credit which permits any amount not utilized during any of the specified periods to be carried over and added to the amounts available in subsequent periods.

- *Letter of credit (Non-Cumulative)* – A revolving letter of credit which prohibits the amount not utilized during the specific period to be available in the subsequent periods.

- *Letter of credit (Deferred Payment)* – A letter of credit issued for the purchase and financing of merchandise, similar to acceptance letter of credit, except that it requires presentation

L

of sight drafts which are payable on installment basis usually for periods of 1 year or more. Under this type of credit, the seller is financing the buyer until the stipulated time his drafts can be presented to the bank for payment. There is a significant deference in the bank's commitment, depending on whether the negotiating bank advised or confirmed the letter of credit.

- *Letter of credit (McLean)* – A letter of credit which requires the beneficiary to present only a draft or a receipt for specified funds before he receives payment.

- *Letter of credit (Negotiable)* – A letter of credit issued in such form that it allows any bank to negotiate the documents. Negotiable credits incorporate the opening bank's engagement, stating that the drafts will be duly honored on presentation, provided they comply with ail terms of the credit. A negotiable letter of credit says specifically that the "Drafts must be negotiated or presented to the drawee not later than..." In contrast, the straight letter of credit does not mention the word "negotiated."

- *Letter of credit (Revolving)* – A credit which includes a provision for reinstating its face value after being drawn under within a stated period of time. This kind of credit facilitates the financing of ongoing regular purchases.

- *Letter of credit (Standby)* – One issued for the express purpose of effecting payment in the event of default. The issuing bank is prepared to pay but does not expect to as long as the underlying transaction is properly fulfilled.

- *Letter of credit (traveler's)* – A letter of credit which is issued by a bank to a customer preparing for an extended trip. The customer pays for the letter of credit at the time of issuance, and a bank issues the letter for a specified period of time in the amount purchased. The bank furnishes a list of correspondent banks where drafts against the letter of credit will be honored. The bank also identifies the customer by exhibiting a specimen signature of the purchaser in the folder enclosing the list of correspondent banks. Each bank, which honors a draft, endorses on the letter of credit the date when a payment was made, the bank's name, the amount drawn against the letter of credit, and charges the issuing bank's account.

LC   Line of Credit

A bank's commitment to make loans to a particular customer up to a specified maximum amount during a specified time period.

L

LCE **Latest Cost Estimate**

Accounting and Business term for most recent cost estimate on a specified item or project.

LCM **Lower of Cost or Market**

Business term for the basis on which a price is set being either the actual cost of the product or the prevailing market price, whichever is lower.

LCO **Lowest Cost of Ownership**

Business term for the lowest negotiable price for owning an asset based on specified variables.

LDR **Ledger**

Australian acronym for final book of accounting entry.

LE **Latest Estimate**

Most recent estimate of price on specified goods or services.

LEI **Leading Economic Indicators**

The economic series of indicators that tend to predict future changes in economic activity; officially called Composite Index of 11 Leading Indicators. This series is published monthly by the U.S. Department of Commerce, including average work week, average weekly initial claims, index of net business formation, new orders, and stock prices. The index of leading indicators, the components of which are adjusted for inflation, has an excellent track record of forecasting ups and downs in the business cycle.

LESOP **Leveraged Employee Stock Ownership Plan**

Business term for an employee stock ownership plan (ESOP) in which employee pension and profit-sharing plans borrow money to purchase stock in the company.

LESS **Least Cost Estimating and Scheduling System**

Business planning model that aims to schedule use of resources at minimal costs.

LGR **Leasehold Ground Rent**

Real estate term for the rental income earned by leased unimproved land.

LIBOR **London Interbank Offered Rate**

The most prominent of the *interbank offered rates*, the rate of interest at which banks in London lend funds to other prime banks in London. LIBOR is frequently used as a basis for determining the rate of interest payable on Eurodollars and other Eurocurrency loans. The effective rate of interest on these Eurocredits is LIBOR plus a markup negotiated between lender and borrower. The rate, however, varies according to circumstances – at which funds can be borrowed in particular currencies, amounts, and maturities in the market.

LIFFE **London International Financial Futures and Options Exchange**

A futures exchange based in London. LIFFE is now part of NYSE Euronext following its takeover by Euronext in January 2002 and Euronext's merger with New York Stock Exchange in April 2007.

LIFO **Last In, First Out**

A system of inventory valuation under which the cost of goods sold equals the cost of the latest inventory purchases and a firm computes the ending inventory cost from the costs of the older units. In periods of rising prices and increasing inventories, LIFO leads to higher reported expenses and therefore lower reported income and lower balance sheet inventories than does *FIFO (first in, first out)*. Note: LIFO is not allowed under IFRS.

Example

Assume the following data regarding inventory during the year.

	Units	Unit Cost	Total Cost
Beginning Inventory, October 1	1,000	$5.00	$5,000
Purchases:			
October 3	3,500	6.00	21,000
October 9	4,000	7.00	28,000
October 19	2,000	8.00	16,000
October 25	2,000	9.00	18,000
Total	12,500		$88,000
Number of units in cost of goods available for sale			12,500

L

Number of units sold	10,000
Number of units in ending inventory	2,500

Under LIFO, the year-end inventory valuation and the cost of goods sold are:

Beginning Inventory, October 1	1,000	$5.00	$5,000
October 3	1,500	6.00	9,000
Total	2,500		$14,000
Cost of goods available for sale			$88,000
Less: Ending inventory			14,000
Cost of goods sold			$74,000

See also **FIFO**.

LILO   **Last In, Last Out**

Inventory accounting term.

LINK   **LINK**

The UK's cash machine network.

LISH; LIST
Last In, Still Here; Last In, Still There

Facetious terms as variations on **LIFO** and **FIFO** inventory accounting methods, referring to inventory that hasn't sold as quickly as anticipated.

LL   **Low Load**

Mutual fund investment that is sold for a relatively low sales charge.

LLC   **Limited Liability Corporation**

Type of corporate entity, not available in all 50 of the United States, that combines the tax and legal characteristics of organization as a corporation and as a partnership.

LMM   **Liquid Money Market**

Money-market investment that can be quickly converted to cash.

LMRA **Labor-Management Relations Act**

Also known as Taft-Hartley Act, passed into U.S. law in 1947 and the provisions of which include injunctions against labor strikes.

LN **Lien**

A creditor's claim against an individual's or entity's property or assets.

Loan

Transaction wherein one party allows a second party to use property or assets for a specified period of time, generally in exchange for payment (interest).

Lot Number

Business management term for a group of goods or services assigned a unique number for identification purposes.

LO **Lowest Offer**

Business management term for the smallest amount offered in exchange for goods or services for sale.

LOB **Line of Business**

Descriptor for type of goods or services offered by a business or individual.

LP **Limited Partnership**

Organization established to manage a business or project, composed of general partners to manage the venture and limited partners who invest without liability and without involvement in day-today operations.

Linear Programming

A technique that maximizes a revenue, contribution or profit function, or minimizes a cost function. Linear Programming has two components:

1. Objective function
2. Constraints, including non-negativity constraints, which are typically inequalities.

L

LPS   **Last Period Satisfied**

IRS term as indicator for the most recent tax period for which a taxpayer's obligations are paid in full.

LR   **Low Risk**

Descriptor for project or investment evaluated as holding little possibility of having little or no return on investment.

Loan Rate

Percentage (generally annual) of interest applied to a loan.

LS   **Lump Sum**

Single large payment of money paid or received as opposed to periodic payments.

LSC   **Lump-Sum Contract**

Business agreement setting forth terms for payment or repayment of an obligation in a single amount.

LSD   **Lump-Sum Distribution**

Single payment made to a departing or retiring employee covering pension, salary reduction and/or profit-sharing plans, and to which certain tax rules apply.

LT   **Legal Tender**

Currency that may be lawfully offered or accepted in purchases or in payments of debts.

LTCG   **Long-Term Capital Gain**

Profits on the sale of an asset held for longer than 12 months and subject to long-term capital gain taxes.

LTCL   **Long-Term Capital Loss**

Loss on the sale of an asset held for longer than 12 months and which can for tax purposes be used to offset capital gains and ordinary income.

LTD   **Limited**

A British business formed as a corporation.

L

LTP   **Limit on Tax Preferences**

IRS limitation on amounts of certain items, such as passive losses and depreciation, that can be used as deductions when calculating Alternative Minimum Tax (AMT).

LTV   **Loan to Value Ratio**

Ratio of money borrowed to fair market value of the property involved, usually real estate.

LV   **Land Value**

Real estate term for market value of unimproved land or the underlying land of improved property.

LWOP   **Leave Without Pay**

Business term for approved leave of absence for an employee during which no salary is drawn.

LWP   **Leave With Pay**

Business term for approved leave of absence for an employee during which all or partial salary is drawn.

L

M

M-1 Currency in circulation

Money supply such as commercial bank demand deposits, traveler's checks, credit union share drafts, NOW and automatic transfer from savings (ATS), and mutual savings bank demand deposits.

M-2 M-L Plus All Time-Related Deposits

Components include M-1 plus overnight Eurodollars and repurchase agreements issued by commercial banks, savings accounts, money market mutual fund shares, and time deposits under $100,000.

M-3 M-2 Money supply

Components include M-2 and time deposits over $100,000 and term repurchase agreements.

MA Margin Account

Investment account that allows a customer to buy securities with money borrowed from the broker under certain terms.

M&A Mergers and Acquisitions

Combination of two or more companies (merger) or the takeover by one company of the controlling interest of another (acquisition); specialized area of financial management and consulting.

MACRS Modified Accelerated Cost Recovery System

The accelerated cost recovery system as revised by The Tax Reform Act of 1986. MACRS abandons the concept of useful life and accelerates depreciation deductions by placing all depreciable assets into one of eight age property classes, each of which has a designated pattern of allowable depreciation (double-declining balance, 150% declining balance, or straight-line with a half-year convention). It calculates deductions, based on an allowable percentage of the asset's original cost. This rule is characterized as follows:

1. The concept of useful life is abandoned and depreciation deductions are accelerated by placing all depreciable assets

into one of eight age property classes. It calculates deductions, based on an allowable percentage of the asset's original cost (See Exhibits 1 and 2). With a shorter asset tax life than useful life, the company would be able to deduct depreciation more quickly and save more in income taxes in the earlier years, thereby making an investment more attractive. The rationale behind the system is that this way the government encourages the company to invest in facilities and increase its productive capacity and efficiency.

2. Since the allowable percentages in Exhibit 1 add up to 100%, there is no need to consider the salvage value of an asset in computing depreciation.

3. The company may elect the straight line method. The straight line convention must follow what is called the half year convention. This means that the company can deduct only half of the regular straight line depreciation amount in the first year. The reason for electing to use the MACRS optional straight line method is that some firms may prefer to stretch out depreciation deductions using the straight line method rather than to accelerate them. Those firms are the ones that just start out or have little or no income and wish to show more income on their income statements.

4. If an asset is disposed of before the end of its class life, the half-year convention allows half the depreciation for that year (early disposal rule).

Exhibit 1: Modified Accelerated Cost Recovery System, Classification of Assets
Property class

Year	3-year	5-year	7-year	10-year	15-year	20-year
1	33.3%	20.0%	14.3%	10.0%	5.0%	3.8%
2	44.5	32.0	24.5	18.0	9.5	7.2
3	14.8a	19.2	17.5	14.4	8.6	6.7
4	7.4	11.5a	12.5	11.5	7.7	6.2
5		11.5	8.9a	9.2	6.9	5.7
6		5.8	8.9	7.4	6.2	5.3
7			8.9	6.6a	5.9a	4.9
8			4.5	6.6	5.9	4.5a

Year	3-year	5-year	7-year	10-year	15-year	20-year
9				6.5	5.9	4.5
10				6.5	5.9	4.5
11				3.3	5.9	4.5
12					5.9	4.5
13					5.9	4.5
14					5.9	4.5
15					5.9	4.5
16					3.0	4.4
17						4.4
18						4.4
19						4.4
20						4.4
21						2.2
Total	100%	100%	100%	100%	100%	100%

Exhibit 2: MACRS Tables by Property Class

MACRS Property Class & Depreciation Method	Useful Life (ADR Midpoint Life) "a"	Examples of Assets
3-year property 200% declining balance	4 years or less	Most small tools are included; the law specifically excludes autos and light trucks from this property class.
5-year property 200% computers, declining balance	More than 4 years to Less than 10 years	Autos and light trucks, typewriters, copiers, duplicating equipment, heavy general- purpose trucks, and research and experimentation equipment are included.
7-year property 200% and declining balance	10 years or more to less than 16 years	Office furniture and fixtures, most items of machinery and equipment used in production are included

M

10-year property 200% declining balance	16 years or more to less than 20 years	Various machinery and equipment, such as that used in petroleum distilling and refining and in the milling of grain, are included.
15-year property 150% declining balance	20 years or more to less than 25 years	Sewage treatment plants, telephone and electrical distribution facilities, and land improvements are included.
20-year property 150% declining balance	25 years or more	Service stations and other real property with an ADR midpoint life of less than 27.5 years are included.
27.5-year property Straight-line	Not applicable	All residential rental property is included
31.5-year property Straight-line	Not applicable	All nonresidential property is included.

M&D   Mergers and Divestitures

Combination of two or more companies (merger) or the disposition of the controlling interest of one company by another (divestiture) through outright sale, employee purchase, liquidation, etc.; specialized area of financial management and consulting.

MAF   Master Appraisal File

Real estate term for compilation of key data for appraisals of a certain property type or class in a given area.

MAI   Member, Appraisal Institute

Member of the American Institute of Real Estate Appraisers.

MAS   Management Accounting System

Generic term for computer and related systems directed towards business operations and decision-making.

Management Advisory Services

Business management and consulting services offered by accountants, generally in the areas of computer technology, budgeting, internal controls, operations, planning, human resources and other management decision-making functions.

MB **Megabyte**

Roughly one million bytes.

Merchant Bank

European or U.S. financial institution that offers services that include investment banking, portfolio management, mergers and acquisitions, and accepting deposits generated by bank credit/debit and charge card transactions.

Municipal Bond

Tax-exempt bonds issued by municipalities, usually for public improvement or operating budgets.

MBA **Mortgage Banking Association**
(www.mbaa.org)

A national trade association of people engaged in the mortgage banking business, dedicated to the betterment of the mortgage banking industry through education, legislation, and high ethical standards for its members.

MBB **Mortgage-Backed Bonds**

Securities backed by mortgages. The Government National Mortgage Association (GNMA) guarantees some of the mortgages.

MBE **Management by Exception**

A management concept under which only exceptional or "red flag" events are reported or acted upon. Management can pay attention to those results or occurrences that deviate in some way from that what was expected.

MBI **Management Buy In**

A management buy-in occurs when a management team from outside the company raises the necessary finance, buys it, and becomes the company's new management.

MBO   Management by Objective

A system of performance appraisal having the following characteristics: (1) it is a formal system in that each manager is required to take certain prescribed actions and to complete certain written documents and (2) the manager and subordinates discuss the subordinate's job description, agree to short-term performance targets, discuss the progress made towards meeting these targets, and periodically evaluate the performance and provide the feedback.

Management Buyout

Purchase of all of a company's publicly held shares by existing management, thereby taking the company private.

MBR   Maximum Base Rent

Real estate term for the level above which a property's base rent (excluding add-on fees, etc.) cannot rise during the stated term of the lease.

MBS   Mortgage-Backed Securities

Interchangeable with Mortgage-Backed Bonds (MBB).

MBTI   Myers Briggs Type Indicator

The most popular psychological test for employee development. MBTI consists of more than 100 questions about how the person feels or prefers to behave in different situations. The MBTI identifies individuals' preferences for energy (introversion versus extroversion), information gathering (sensing versus intuition), decision-making (thinking versus feeling), and lifestyle (judging versus perceiving). MBTI is used for understanding such things as communication, motivation, teamwork, work styles, and leadership.

MC   Marginal Cost

Business management term for the change in the total costs of an enterprise as the result of one more or one less unit of output, also called incremental cost. Formula:

$$MC = \frac{\text{Change in total cost}}{\text{Change in quantity}}$$

MCA   **Material Control Adjustment**

Revision of current or planned inventory or production as a means to optimize material purchases.

MCC   **Marginal Cost of Capital**

Analysis that relates a firm's cost of capital to the level of new financing, used to determine the discount rate to be used in the firm's capital budgeting process:

1. Determine the cost and the percentage of financing to be used for each source of capital (e.g., debt, preferred stock, and common stock equity.)

2. Use the following formula to compute the points where the weighted cost will increase:

$$\text{Break point} = \frac{\text{Maximum amount of the lower cost source of capital}}{\text{Percentage of financing provided by the source}}$$

3. Calculate the weighted cost of capital over the range of total financing between break points.

4. Construct a table that shows the weighted cost of capital for each level of total new financing.

MCE   **Manufacturing Cycle Effectiveness**

Business management measure, expressed as a percentage, of the efficacy of a specified manufacturing process.

MD   **Maturity Date**

Investment term for

1. date on which the principal amount of a financial instrument becomes due and payable;

2. date on which an installment loan must be paid in full;

3. average due date of factored receivables.

Memorandum of Deposit

Banking documentation for cash, checks or drafts placed with a financial institution for credit to an account.

Money Down

Down payment on a loan under contract.

MDA   Management Discussion and Analysis

An annual report disclosure that provides an analysis of the results of operations and financial condition.

ME   Math Error

Accounting and IRS term used to indicate where a calculation has been found to contain an arithmetic error.

MERC   Chicago Mercantile Exchange

See CME.

MGN   Margin

Brokerage and investment term for the amount that an investor deposits with a broker when borrowing from the broker to buy securities.

MHA   Man-Hour Accounting

Accounting system that emphasizes labor hours and related costs connected with a specific job or project.

MHZ   Megahertz

The measurement of speed of the transmission of the computer's electronic devices. One MHz represents one million cycles per second. The speed of microprocessors, called the clock speed, is measured in megahertz. For example, a microprocessor that runs at 200 MHz executes 200 million cycles per second.

MIBOR   Madrid Interbank Offered Rate

International banking term.

MIC   Material Inventory Control

Accounting and bookkeeping systems for monitoring material, from raw material to finished goods.

MICR   Magnetic Ink Character Recognition

A magnetic coding imprinted on checks and deposit slips to speed up the check and deposit clearing process.

MIF   Master Inventory File

Accounting and bookkeeping term for primary documents and recordkeeping systems for material inventory.

Mercato Italiano Futures

Italian Futures Market

MIMS **Material Information Management System**

Accounting and management term for computerized and other systems for managing and reporting on the material components of a business.

MIPO **Multiple-Item Purchase Order**

Bookkeeping and management document setting forth the specifications and terms for an order between customer and vendor of more than one item.

MIR **Master Inventory Record**

Accounting and bookkeeping term for primary documents and records for material inventory.

MIRR **Modified Internal Rate of Return**

The discount rate which forces Initial cash outlay = present value of terminal (future) value compounded at the cost of capital. The MIRR forces cash flow reinvestment at the cost of capital rather than the project's own IRR, which was the problem with the IRR.

1. MIRR avoids the problem of multiple IRRs.
2. Conflicts can still occur in ranking mutually exclusive projects with differing sizes. NPV should again be used in such a case. Or the MIRR overcomes this problem.

Example

Assume the following:

Cash Flows

Projects	0	1	2	3	4	5
A	(100)	120				
B	(100)					201.14

Computing IRR and NPV at 10 percent gives the following different rankings:

Projects	IRR	NPV at 10%
A	20%	$ 9.01
B	15	24.90

The difference in ranking between the two methods is caused by the methods' reinvestment rate assumptions. The IRR method assumes Project A's cash inflow of $120 is reinvested at 20% for the subsequent 4 years and the NPV method assumes $120 is reinvested at 10%. The correct decision is to select the project with the higher NPV (Project B), since the NPV method assumes a more realistic reinvestment rate, that is, the cost of capital (10% in this example).

Project A's MIRR is:

First, computer the project's terminal value at a 10% cost of capital.

120 T1(10%, 4 years) = 120 x 1.4641 = 175.69

Next, find the IRR by setting:

100 = 175.69 T3(MIRR, 5 years)

T3 = 100/175.69 = 0.5692, which gives MIRR = about 12%

Now we see the consistent ranking from both the NPV and MIRR methods.

	MIRR	NPV at 10%
A	12%	$ 9.01
B	15	24.90

Note

Microsoft Excel has a function MIRR(values, finance_rate, reinvest_rate).

MIS **Management Information Systems**

A computer-based or manual system which transforms data into information useful in the support of decision making. MIS can be classified as performing three functions:

1. MIS that generates reports. These reports can be financial statements, inventory status reports or performance reports that are needed for routine and non-routine purposes.

2. MIS that answer "what-if" kinds of questions asked by management. For example, questions such as "what would happen to cash flow if the company changes its credit term for its customers?" can be answered by MIS. This type of MIS can be called Simulation or What-If model.

3. MIS supports decision making. This type of MIS is appropriately called Decision Support System (DSS). DSS

attempts to integrate the decision maker, the data base, and the quantitative models being used.

Marketing Information System

A process for making marketing decisions using computers, in which marketing information is collected, analyzed, and disseminated or distributed. Exhibit 1 shows the inputs, subsystems, and outputs of a typical MIS.

MIT   **Market-If-Touched Order**

A contingent buy/sell order of securities at market price if execution of another order is placed at a given price.

Municipal Investment Trust

Investment trust that buys municipal bonds and passes the tax-free income on to shareholders.

MLP   **Master Limited Partnership**

Public limited partnership composed of certain types of corporate assets or private limited partnerships, especially used for real estate or oil and gas ventures.

MLS   **Multiple Listing Service**

Association of real estate agents who agree to share property listings with one another and share commissions among two or more agents who participate in a completed transaction.

MM   **Money Market**

Market for short-term debt instruments.

MMDA   **Money Market Deposit Account**

Highly liquid, market-sensitive bank account available since 1982, with an interest rate generally comparable to rates on money-market mutual funds, and insured by the Federal Deposit Insurance Corporation.

MMF   **Money Market Fund**

Open-ended mutual fund that invests in highly liquid and safe securities and pays commensurate interest rates.

MMMF Money Market Mutual Fund

Interchangeable with but less often used than Money Market Fund (MMF).

MNC   Multinational Corporation

A company operating in two or more countries. Its ownership is in only one country. Special features of a multinational corporation (MNC) are as follows:

1. *Multiple-currency problem.* Sales revenues may be collected in one currency, assets denominated in another, and profits measured in a third.

2. *Various legal, institutional, and economic constraints.* There are variations in such things as tax laws, labor practices, balance of payment policies, and government controls with respect to the types and sizes of investments, types and amount of capital raised, and repatriation of profits.

3. *Internal control problem.* When the parent office of a multinational company and its affiliates are widely located, internal organizational difficulties arise.

MNE   Multinational Enterprise

Business entity conducting business internationally. *See also* **MNC**.

MOI   Minimum Operating Inventory

Lowest or smallest amount of material needed to maintain a business or a certain process.

MONEP Marche des Options Negociables de Paris

Subsidiary of Paris Bourse, the national stock market of France.

MOP   Margin of Profit

Accounting and business term for net sales less cost of goods, the relationship between gross profits and net sales.

MP   Market Price

Price agreed upon by willing buyers and sellers of a product or service as determined by supply and demand. In brokerage last reported price at which a security was sold on an exchange.

M/P   Mail Payment

Bookkeeping indicator of how a payment was or will be made or received.

MRP   Material Requirement Planning

A computer-based information system designed to handle ordering and scheduling of dependent-demand inventories (such as raw materials, component parts, and subassemblies, which will be used in the production of a finished product). MRP begins with a schedule for finished goods which is converted into a schedule of requirements for the subassemblies, component parts, and raw materials which will be needed to produce the finished items in the specified time frame. Thus, MRP is designed to answer three questions: what is needed, how much is needed, and when it is needed. The primary inputs of MRP are a bill of materials, which tells of what a finished product is composed, a master schedule, which tells how much finished product is desired and when, and an inventory-records file, which tells how much inventory is on hand or on order. This information is processed using various computer programs to determine the net requirements for each period of the planning horizon. Outputs from the process include planned-order schedules, order releases, changes, performance-control reports, planning reports, and exception reports.

MRP II   Manufacturing Resource Planning

Integrated information system that steps beyond first-generation MRP to synchronize all aspects (not just manufacturing) of the business, including production, sales, inventories, schedules, and cash flows. MRP-II uses an MPS (master production schedule), which is a statement of the anticipated manufacturing schedule for selected items for selected periods. MRP also uses the MPS. Thus, MRP is a component of an MRP-II system.

MSA   Metropolitan Statistical Area

1. A city having a population of at least 50,000.
2. An urbanized area with a population in excess of 50,000 with a total metropolitan population of at least 100,000.

MSCI EAFE
Morgan Stanley Capital International Europe Australia Far East Index

The index tracks the performance of all major stock markets outside of North America. It is market-weighted and is composed of 1,041 companies. It is the major index used by investors to see how U.S. shares are performing against other markets worldwide. *See also* **EAFE**.

MTM   Methods-Time Measurement

System of predetermined motion-time data used to develop standards for highly repetitive tasks.

MTN   Medium-Term Note

Note with a maturity of two to ten years.

MTR   Marginal Tax Rate

Tax rate paid on the last dollar of income earned; the highest tax rate paid.

MTSR   Mid-Term Status Report

Management report produced at the halfway point of a financial reporting period or a project's completion timeline, scheduled to evaluate the condition of the project.

MU   Markup

Cost difference between a retailer's costs for a product or service and what the retailer charges customers.

MUD   Mixed Use Development

Real estate term for property planned and/or zoned for different types of buildings, *e.g.*, residential and commercial.

Municipal Utility District

Political subdivision within a municipality that provides utility-related services and may issue special assessment bonds.

MUNIS   Municipal Bonds

Bonds issued by local governments and their agencies on which interest is exempt from federal income taxation, provided they qualify as public purpose bonds; simply called *munis*. Interest may also be exempt from state and local income taxation in the state of issue.

Note

You may consider municipal bonds for tax or income reasons. If you do, you may face three investment choices for diversification:

1. buying them on your own,
2. muni unit investment trust (UIT), and

3. muni mutual funds. If the preservation of capital is of primary importance, the UIT may be a better investment than a mutual fund. Figure 1 compares aspects of the three approaches.

MURB   Multi-Unit Residential Building

Canadian real estate term for apartment building.

MV   Market Value

Theoretical highest price that a willing buyer would pay for a product or service, and lowest price that a willing seller would accept, both parties acting fully informed and intelligently.

MVA   Market Value Added

The difference between the market value of a firm's capital (equity and debt) and the amount of capital that shareholders and debtholders have invested in the firm.

MWL   Minimum Wage Laws

Federal legislation that sets forth the lowest fixed wage payable to employees of various groups.

MXD   Mixed Use District

Real estate term for land planned and/or zoned for a variety of uses, *e.g.*, residential and commercial.

MXN   Mexican Peso

Unit of currency in Mexico

MYR   Malaysian Ringgit

Unit of currency in Malaysia

N

NA   **Net Assets**
Total assets of a business less liabilities.

Not Applicable or Not Available
Used in many contexts as indicator of information, material or product either unavailable or irrelevant.

NABE   **National Association of Business Economists**
(www.nabe.com)
Conducts a survey on the future economic condition of the nation.

NADS   **Net After Debt Service**
Gross profit less annual debt service (ADS).

NAFTA   **North American Free Trade Agreement**
The agreement among the United States, Canada, and Mexico, signed in 1992 and ratified in 1993, that seeks to eliminate all trade barriers over 10 years. It took effect January 1994. Many economists believe the three nations are likely to gain jobs from increased trade.

NAHB   **National Association of Home Builders**
(www.nahb.com)
A trade association that helps promote the policies that make housing a national priority. Its membership consists of single, multifamily and commercial home builders. The NAHB serves as a public interest group to support legislation for the home building industry

NAM   **National Association of Manufacturers**
(www.nam.org)
The nation's largest industrial trade association The NAM represents 14,000 members (including 10,000 small and mid-sized companies) and 350 member associations serving manufacturers and employees in every industrial sector and all 50 states. Headquartered in Washington, D.C., the NAM has 10 additional offices across the country. The NAM was founded in Cincinnati,

Ohio in 1895. Fortune magazine rates the NAM as one of the 10 most influential advocacy groups in the United States.

NAR   National Association of Realtors
(www.realtor.com)

Founded in 1908 and located in Chicago, IL, a federation of 50 state associations and 1,848 local real estate boards, termed either Realtors or Realtor-Associates. With over 800,000 members, the National Association of Realtors promotes education, professional standards, and updates brokerage appraisal techniques, property management and land development practices, industrial real estate and farm brokerage, and counseling methods.

NAREIT National Association of Real Estate Investment Trusts
(www.reit.com)

Trade organization representing the interests of those involved in Real Estate Investment Trusts. It is the worldwide representative voice for REITs and publicly traded real estate companies with an interest in U.S. real estate and capital markets. NAREIT's members are REITs and other businesses throughout the world that own, operate, and finance income-producing real estate, as well as those firms and individuals who advise, study, and service those businesses.

NASD   National Association of Securities Dealers

New-York based organization for standards and ethical behavior composed of investment banking firms and supervised by the Securities Exchange Commission (SEC). NASD monitors the over-the-counter (OTC) market.

NASDAQ
National Association of Securities Dealers Automated Quotations System
(www.nasdaq.com)

Computerized system owned by NASD, listing prices for over-the-counter securities. NASDAQ currently lists over 5,500 stocks with a total market capitalization of over $1.6 trillion.

NAV   Net Asset Value

Market value of a mutual fund share. NAV is measured as follows:

$$NAV = \frac{\text{Fund's total assets} - \text{Liabilities}}{\text{Number of shares outstanding in the fund}}$$

For example, let's look at AAA mutual fund:

AAA Mutual Fund	Market Value
Value of the portfolio	$38,000
Minus total liabilities	$12,000
Net Value	$26,000
Number of shares outstanding	2,000
NAV per share ($26,000, 2,000)	$13.00

To determine the value of an investment assuming 5% or 100 shares of the fund's outstanding shares are owned, simple multiply the NAV by the number of shares held. Thus, the value of the investment is:

$13.00 × 100 = $1,300

NB   Nonbusiness

Tax-accounting indicator for personal as opposed to business-related income or expenses.

NBER   National Bureau of Economic Research
(*www.nber.org*)

Publishers of the Business Conditions Digest. The bureau analyzes and selects the time series data based on each series' ability to be identified as a leading, coincident or lagging indicator over several decades of aggregate economic activity. The Digest can be used to understand past economic behavior and to forecast future economic activity with a high degree of accuracy.

NBR   Nightly Business Report

Television program that provides consumer, business and financial news.

NC   No Charge

Accounting and bookkeeping term to indicate waiver of all or certain parts of costs for a product or service.

Noncollectable

Accounting and bookkeeping term to indicate an invoice or receivable amount that the business has unsuccessfully attempted to collect and subsequently determined to be lost.

NCI   No-Cost Item

Business inventory item with no or insignificant cost to the business and/or given to customers at no charge.

No Currency Involved

International transaction in which no money was exchanged between the parties.

NCV   No Commercial Value

Business product, service or commodity determined to have no current value in any market.

ND   National Debt

Economics term for all debt owned by a federal government.

Net Debt

Finance term for total debt owed by an individual or business entity.

Next Day

Indicator of requirement for next day delivery of stock certificates, and for settlement (payment) on that same day.

NDB   Net Debt Balance

Finance term for total current unpaid principal amount on a loan.

NE   Net Earnings

Finance term for income remaining after all expenses have been paid or deducted.

NF   No Funds

Banking and bookkeeping indicator for an account with no current deposits.

NFA   National Futures Association
(www.nfa.futures.org)

The industrywide, self-regulatory organization for the U.S. futures industry.

NICS **Newly Industrialized Countries**

Economics term for nations recently converted and/or newly introduced to methods and aims of industrialization.

NIF **Note Issuance Facility**

Facility provided by a syndicate of banks allowing borrowers to issue short-term notes that are placed by the syndicate in the eurocurrency markets.

NIS **Not In Stock**

Inventory management term for product or item not currently available for use or purchase.

NL **No Load**

Mutual fund with no commission or sales charge.

NNN **Triple Net**

A lease that includes, in addition to the basic rent, a share of the real property taxes, insurance, and maintenance. Triple-net-leases are standard in commercial property leases for shopping centers and malls.

NOI **Net Operating Income**

Gross income from operating a property or business less operating expenses, but before deducting income taxes and financing expenses.

NOL **Net Operating Loss**

Accounting term for excess of business expenses over income in a tax year.

NOP **Non-Operating**

Business and accounting term for any source of income or expense other than direct operation function of the business.

NOW **Negotiable Order of Withdrawal Account**

Bank or savings and loan account on which negotiable withdrawal drafts can be written; an interest-bearing checking account.

N

NP   Nonprofit, Not-for-Profit

Organization exempt from corporate income taxes, generally operated for charitable, humanitarian or educational purposes, and to which donations are tax-deductible by the donor.

Notary Public

Public officer or other person authorized to authenticate contracts, acknowledge deeds, take affidavits, etc.

Notes Payable

Finance term for a written promise to pay a specified amount to a certain entity on demand or on a specified date, reflected as a liability on the financial statement.

NPO   Nonprofit Corporations

Formed under another state law (sometimes for specific purposes set by statutes), these corporations are not established to earn a profit (so no exclusive distribution to its members, directors, or officers) but to meet a charitable, educational, or scientific purpose. They have no shareholders and no dividends.

NPR   Net Patient Revenue

Gross in-patient revenue (in hospital) plus gross outpatient revenue minus related deductions from revenue.

NPV   Net Present Value

Investment analysis method of determining whether performance of a proposed investment will be adequate for the investor's objectives. The present value (PV) of all cash inflows from the investment is compared to the initial investment. Formula:

$$NPV = PV - I$$

If the result is an NPV > 1, an investment is worthy of consideration.

NR; N/R
Not Rated

Indicator used by securities rating services and mercantile agencies for securities or companies that have not been rated, and having neither a positive nor negative implication.

N

N/R   **Notes Receivable**

Finance term for a written promise to receive payment of a specified amount on demand or on a specified date, reflected as an asset on the financial statement.

NRA   **Net Rentable Area**

Real estate term for that portion of space in a building or project that may be rented to tenants and upon which rental payments are based.

NRV   **Net Realizable Value**

Method of valuing realizable assets of a company less liabilities

NSCC   **National Securities Clearing Corporation**
(www.nscc.com)

Organization through which brokerage firms, exchanges and other clearing corporations reconcile accounts with each other.

NSF   **Not Sufficient Funds**

Draft or note not payable because the account on which it is drawn has insufficient funds to cover the amount written.

NT   **Net Tax**

Total tax owed after all deductions, exemptions and adjustments to income.

N/T   **Net Terms**

Amount owed after all relevant deductions have been taken from the gross amount.

NTA   **Net Tangible Assets**

Total assets of a company less any intangible assets, *e.g.,* goodwill, patents and trademarks, and less all liabilities.

NTDB   **National Trade Data Bank**

An international trade data bank compiled by 15 U.S. Government agencies. The data bank contains the latest census data on U.S. imports and exports by commodity and country, the complete CIA *World Factbook,* and current market research among others.

N

NVS   Non-Voting Stock

Securities that do not empower the holder to vote on corporate resolutions or the election of directors.

NW   Net Worth

The value of all assets of an individual or organization minus any debts.

NWC   Net Working Capital

Current assets minus current liabilities.

NYSE New York Stock Exchange

(www.nyse.com)

Also called the *Big Board* and *The Exchange,* the NYSE was established in 1792 and is the oldest and largest stock exchange in the U.S.

NZD   New Zealand Dollar

Currency of New Zealand

NZICA New Zealand Institute of Chartered Accountants

NZICA is the membership body of choice for over 33,000 accounting and business professionals, working around New Zealand and across the globe.

N

OA Office Audit

Accounting term for a professional examination and verification of accounts and records and supporting data, and a report or statement of the results of the examination, for an individual office of a company.

Old Account

Account inactive but kept open.

On Account

Accounting term for the partial payment of an obligation; an informal transaction in which a buyer agrees to make payment at some time after goods are delivered.

Open Account

Accounting term for a credit account with an unpaid balance.

OAC On Approved Credit

Goods or services delivered based on the customer's credit previously approved by the vendor.

OB Obligation Bond

Mortgage bond in which the face value exceeds the value of the underlying property, and the difference compensates the lender for its costs exceeding the mortgage value.

Operating Budget

Estimate of revenue and expenditure involving the direct operation of an enterprise for a specified period.

Organizational Behavior

The actions and attitudes of people in organizations. The field of organizational behavior (OB) is the body of knowledge derived from these actions and attitudes. It can help managers understand the complexity within organizations, identify problems, determine how to correct them, and establish whether the changes would make a difference.

Out of Business

Indicator of client or customer that has ceased operation.

OBL **Outstanding Balance List**

Accounting report listing all unpaid amounts in a certain time period and/or for a certain division.

OBS **Off Balance Sheet**

Is a process when an asset or debt or financing activity not on the company's balance sheet

OC **Open Contract**

Agreement whose terms have not been fully negotiated, executed or completed.

OCC **Options Clearing Corporation**
(www.optionsclearing.com)

Corporation owned by stock exchanges, handling options transactions.

OCF **Operating Cash Flow**

The cash flow amount used to represent the money moving through a company as a result of its operations, as opposed to its purely financial transactions.

OCI **Other Comprehensive Income**

Part of total comprehensive income but is generally excluded from net income.

Examples of items that may be classified in other comprehensive income are:

• Unrealized holding gains or losses on investments that are classified as available for sale

• Foreign currency translation gains or losses

• Pension plan gains or losses

• Pension prior service costs or credits

OCR **Optical Character Recognition**

The software that involves reading text from paper and translating the images into a form that the computer can manipulate.

OD   **Overdraft, Overdrawn**

Extension of credit by a lending institution on a draft or check written on an account.

OE   **Operating Expense**

Expenditure directly related to producing a product or service.

OEBS   **Office of Employee Benefits Security**
(www.dol.gov/EBSA)

U.S. Department of Labor subsidiary.

OECD   **Organization for Economic Cooperation and Development**
(www.oecd.org)

An organization addresses issues of mutual concern with a view of expanding foreign trade, economic growth, and employment. The organization is composed of countries including the United States, England, France, Germany, Canada, Japan, Greece, and Australia.

OEIT   **Open-End Investment Trust**

Trust that continually creates new investment shares on demand.

OEX   **Options Exchange**

Location where option securities are traded.

OFLT   **Office of Foreign Labor and Trade**

U.S. Department of Commerce subsidiary.

OI   **Operating Income**

Revenue directly related to the product or service that a business offers.

OID   **Original Issue Discount**

Bond bought at a deep discount, also called a Zero-Coupon Bond. The interest is added to the principal semiannually and both the principal and the accumulated interest are paid at maturity.

OJT   **On-the-Job Training**

Training that transpires at the job site, usually supervised by a manager or an experienced coworker.

OL **Operating Leverage**

A measure of operating risk that arises from fixed operating costs. A simple indication of operating leverage is the effect that a change in sales has on operating income. The formula is:

$$\frac{\text{Operating leverage}}{\text{At a given level of sales}} = \frac{\text{Percent change in operating income}}{\text{Percent change in sales}}$$

$$\text{Or} = \frac{(\text{unit selling price} - \text{unit variable cost}) \times \text{sales}}{(\text{unit selling price} - \text{unit variable cost}) \times \text{sales} - \text{fixed costs}}$$

Example

Assume a unit selling price of $25, a unit variable cost of $15, and fixed costs of $50,000. The company is selling 6,000 units per year.

Its operating leverage is

$$\frac{(\$25 - \$15)(6,000)}{(\$25 - \$15)(6,000) - \$50,000} = \frac{\$60,000}{\$10,000} = 6$$

which means if sales increase by 10 percent, the company can expect its income to increase six times that amount, or 60 percent.

Operating leverage may also be measured by the ratio of fixed operating costs to total costs. A higher ratio indicates greater risk.

Operating Loss

The difference between the revenues of a business and the related costs and expenses, excluding income derived from sources other than regular activities and before income deductions, where costs and expenses exceed revenues.

OLTP **On-Line Transaction Processing**

Systems involved in electronic processing of investment sales and purchases.

OM **Operations Management**

Design, operation, and improvement of the productions/operations system that creates the firm's primary products or services; also called *production/operations management*.

Options Market

Aggregate of people and exchanges involved in buying and selling options securities.

OMB   Office of Management and Budget
(www.whitehouse.gov/omb)

An agency within the Executive Office of the President. The OMB has broad financial management power as well as the responsibility of preparing the executive budget. Among the other duties assigned OMB are: (1) to study and recommend to the President changes relative to the existing organizational structure of the agencies, their activities and methods of business, etc., (2) to apportion appropriations among the agencies and establish reserves in anticipation of cost savings, contingencies, etc., and (3) to develop programs and regulations for improved data gathering pertaining to the Government and its agencies.

OMO   Ordinary Money Order

Financial instrument that can be easily converted into cash by the payee named on the order.

O*NET Occupational Information Network
(http://online.onetcenter.org)

A network that the U.S. Department of Labor replaced the Dictionary of Occupational Titles (DOT) in 1998 with because jobs in the new economy were so qualitatively different from jobs in the old economy, and the DOT no longer served its purpose. The O*NET system serves as the nation's primary source of occupational information, providing comprehensive information on key attributes and characteristics of workers and occupations. The O*NET database houses this data and O*NET OnLine provides easy access to that information. Instead of relying on fixed job titles and narrow task descriptions, the O*NET uses a common language that generalizes across jobs to describe the abilities, work styles, work activities, and work context required for various occupations that are more broadly defined. The following is O*NET OnLine site.

OPBU   Operating Budget

Estimate of revenue and expenditure involving the direct operation of an enterprise for a specified period.

O/PD   Overpaid

Indicator for an amount paid exceeding the amount due or billed.

OPM **Other People's Money**

The use of borrowed funds by individuals to increase the return on an invested capital. Examples are a mortgage to buy real estate and buying stock on margin.

Options Pricing Model

An option pricing model, developed in 1973 by Fischer Black and Myron Scholes, used to price OTC options and value option portfolios. The five factors determining the premium of an option's market value over its expiration value are:

1. Time to maturity
2. Stock price volatility
3. Exercise price
4. Stock price
5. Risk-free rate

OR **Operations Research**

Often used interchangeably with *management science* or *quantitative methods*, a scientific method of providing the decision maker with a quantitative basis for decisions regarding the operations under his/her control. Operations research (OR) is divided broadly into two categories of techniques (models): *optimization models* (mathematical programming) and *simulation models*. Optimization models attempt to provide an optimal solution (or prescriptive solution) to a problem, while simulation models produce a descriptive (or "what-if" type of) solution. It, for example, covers such quantitative techniques as inventory models, linear programming, queuing theory, Program Evaluation and Review Technique (PERT), and Monte Carlo simulation.

O/S **Outstanding**

Accounting and bookkeeping indicator of financial or other obligation unfulfilled.

OSHA **Occupational Safety and Health Act**

Federal legislation of 1970 regarding employers' responsibilities for safety and health in the workplace.

OSI **Out of Stock, Indefinite**

Indicator of a product or inventory item unavailable for an undetermined period of time but not discontinued.

OST   **Out of Stock, Temporary**

Indicator of a product or inventory item unavailable but due to be restocked.

OT   **Overtime**

Time during which an employee worked before or after regularly scheduled working times, pay for which is at the employee's regular hourly wage.

OTC   **Over the Counter**

Securities that are not listed and traded on a national exchange, but are traded electronically through brokers; sometimes called the Third Market.

OTP   **Overtime Premium**

Time during which an employee worked before or after regularly scheduled working times, pay for which is higher than the employee's regular hourly wage.

OTS   **Office of Thrift Supervision**

(www.ots.treas.gov)

U.S. Treasury Department subsidiary established in 1989. The OTS supervises a national thrift industry that is built on the bedrock of the American dream of homeownership—supplying affordable home financing for Americans from all walks of life. The industry has a long history dating back to 1831 with the establishment

P

PA **Public Accountant**

Accountant offering services to the public at large as opposed to one employed on a full-time basis by a company, but not having met statutory and licensing requirements to obtain certification as a CPA.

Purchasing Agent

Individual carrying out the function in a company of managing purchases of goods and services and relationships with vendors, to maintain compliance with company standards and obtain economies of scale and other advantages.

PAC **Pre Authorized Check**

A check written by the payee on the payor's account and deposited on the agreed date.

PAD **Pre Authorized Debit**

Authorization given by the customer to the seller to routinely and automatically charge his or her account.

P&I **Principal and Interest**

Indicates that an amount paid includes both repayment of principal and interest per the lending terms.

PAL **Passive Activity Loss**

Loss produced by investment activities (such as a limited partnership) in which the investor does not materially participate, carrying certain tax consequences.

Pre-Approved Loan

Lending arrangement in which the borrower has been qualified by the lender to obtain a loan of certain terms within a certain time period.

PAM **Pledged Account Mortgage**

Real estate mortgage loan in which part of the down-payment funds are "pledged" to the lender and placed in an interest-bearing account, and drawn from over time to help pay down the mortgage.

PAP   Pre-Arranged Payments

Schedule agreed upon between a customer and vendor or borrower and lender by which certain payments occur automatically.

PAQ   Position Analysis Questionnaire

A standardized job analysis questionnaire containing 194 items representing work behaviors, work conditions, or job characteristics that are generalizable across a wide variety of jobs.

PAT   Pre-Arranged Transfers

Schedule agreed upon between two or more parties by which funds or materials are moved among accounts automatically in order to accomplish stated objectives.

PBGC   Pension Benefit Guaranty Corporation

Federal corporation that guarantees basic pension benefits in covered plans by administering terminated plans and placing liens on corporate assets for certain pension liabilities that were not funded.

PBP   Pay-Back Period

Amount of time required for the cumulative estimated future income from an investment to equal the amount initially invested.

PBR   Price to Book Value Ratio

Ratio of the market value of a company's stock to its tangible net worth.

PC   Plus Commissions

Indicator that a specified amount does not include commission fees.

Petty Cash

Small cash fund maintained by a business for paying minor expenses such as office supplies, delivery gratuities, etc.

PCA   Personal Cash Allowance

Amount budgeted for an individual's discretionary expenses such as entertaining.

PCAOB Public Company Accounting Oversight Board
(www.pcaobus.com)

Established in 2002 as a result of the Sarbanes-Oxley Act, a private sector, non-profit corporation set up to oversee the audits of public companies and ensure that accountancy firms should no longer derive non-audit revenue streams, such as consultancy, from their audit clients.

PCEPI Personal Consumption Expenditure Price Index

A measure of inflation preferred by the Federal Reserve. It is a measure of price changes in consumer goods and services. It consists of the actual and imputed expenditures of households, and includes data pertaining to durables, non-durables, and services. This measure (year 2000=100) excludes food and energy costs.

PCS Preferred Capital Stock

Generally referred to simply as Preferred Stock, a class of stock that pays dividends usually at a fixed rate and that has priority over common stock in the receipt of dividend income and liquidation of assets, and which generally does not carry voting rights.

PD Past Due

Indicator of an invoice or other indebtedness unpaid as of its due date as specified in the credit terms.

Per Diem

Daily allowance, usually for incidental expenses while traveling for business.

Post-Dated

Check, letter, invoice, document, etc., dated later than the date on which it was actually written.

PDA Payroll Deduction Authorization

Documentation between an employee and employer setting forth one-time or ongoing deductions from salary or wages for, *e.g.*, tax withholding, employee benefits, etc.

Personal Digital Assistant

Little portable device for electronic computing purposes. It has a variety of features including wireless communications to phones or computers.

PDCA Plan-Do-Check Act Cycle

"Management by fact" or scientific method approach to continuous improvement (the Deming Wheel). PDCA creates a process-centered environment because it involves studying the current process, collecting and analyzing data to identify causes of problems, planning for improvement, and deciding how to measure improvement (Plan). The plan is then implemented on a small scale if possible (Do). The next step is to determine what happened (Check). If the experiment was successful, the plan is fully implemented (Act). The cycle is then repeated using what was learned from the preceding cycle.

PDD Past Due Date

Indicator or payment received after due date or remaining unpaid after due date.

PDE (Tape)
Price-Dividend-Earnings Tape

Contains monthly data on per share performance. One of the CompuStat tapes developed by Investors Management Science Company, a subsidiary of Standard & Poor's Corporation.

PDI Personal Disposable Income

Individual income in excess of needs for living expenses and taxes, and therefore discretionary for investment, entertainment, etc.

PE Period Ending

Accompanied by a date, indicates termination date of a specified financial reporting, interest-earning, or billing period.

P/E. PER
Price/Earnings Ratio

Also called *earnings multiple*, the P/E ratio represents the amount investors are willing to pay for each dollar of the firm's earnings. A high multiple shows that investors are positive on the firm. The formula is:

$$\text{Price/earnings ratio} = \frac{\text{Market price per share}}{\text{Earnings per share}}$$

For example, assume the following:

- Firm's market price on Dec. 31, 2X12 = $14.00 and earnings per share = $1.80
- Firm's market price on Dec. 31, 2X13 = $28.00 and earnings per share = $2.10

Then:

$$P/E\ 2X12 = \frac{\$14.00}{\$1.80} = 7.78$$

$$PE\ 2X13 = \frac{\$28.00}{\$2.10} = 13.35$$

Thus, investors are showing a higher opinion of the firm in 2X13.

PED   **Period End Date**

Indicates last calendar date of a specified financial reporting or billing period.

PEFCO   **Private Export Funding Corporation**

(www.pefco.com)

Established with U.S. Government support, PEFCO is a private corporation that help finance U.S. exports. Private capital is raised to fund export big-ticket items by American firms by purchasing medium- to long-term debt obligations of importers of U.S. goods at fixed interest rates.

PEP   **Paperless Electronic Payment**

Indicator of payment made generally by telephone or computer, often automatically on a specified due date, and without cash or check.

PERCS   **Preferred Equity—Redemption Cumulative Stock**

Form of preferred stock that allows holders of shares of common stock to exchange common stock for preferred shares, thereby retaining a higher dividend rate.

PERKS   **Perquisites**

Various forms of executive compensation, such as corporate jets, fancy offices, company cars, entertainment expenses, company

P

credit cards, support staff, club memberships, cellular phones, sport tickets, and the like. These are part of a firm's *agency costs*.

PERLS Principal Exchange-Rate-Linked Securities

U.S. debt instrument that pays interest with principal repayment linked to performance of the U.S. dollar vs. foreign currency.

PERT Program Evaluation and Review Technique

A useful management tool for planning, coordinating, and controlling large complex projects such as formulation of a master budget, construction of buildings, installation of computers, and scheduling the closing of books. The development and initial application of PERT was done in connection with the development of the Polaris submarine by the U.S. Navy in the late 1950s. The PERT technique involves the diagrammatical representation of the sequence of activities comprising a project by means of a network consisting of arrows and circles (nodes). Questions to be answered by PERT include:

• When will the project be finished?

• What is the probability that the project will be completed by any given time?

See also CPM.

PEST Political, Economic, Social and Technological analysis

Is an analysis of environmental factors used in the environmental review of a strategic management plan.

PF Pension Fund

Fund established by a corporation or other organization to pay post-retirement non-wage benefits to employees or their designated beneficiaries.

pf Preferred Stock

Class of capital stock that pays dividends at a specified rate and that has preference over common stock in the payment of dividends and liquidation of assets, but that generally does not have voting rights.

PFI Private Finance Initiative

A way of creating public–private partnerships by funding public capital projects with private capital.

PFP **Personal Financial Planning**

A field of financial planning for individuals. It involves (1) analyzing a client's personal finances and (2) recommending how to improve the client's financial condition. Personal financial planning covers the following specific areas:

Analysis of current financial	Long-term accumulation plans
Position	Investment strategies
Life insurance	Estate planning
Tax planning	Cash flow analysis
Disability insurance	Retirement income

PGIM **Potential Gross Income Multiplier**

Ratio of the value of a piece of real estate to the income the property could potentially generate, used as a rule-of-thumb indicator of the property's viability as an investment.

PI **Personal Income**

Income received by an individual from all sources.

Prime Interest Rate

Base rate used by banks in pricing commercial loans to their most creditworthy customers, generally used as a bellwether rate throughout the lending community.

Profitability Index

The present value of an investment's expected cash-flow stream divided by the investment's initial cash outlay.

PIG **Passive Income Generator**

Investment vehicle intended to generate passive income (*i.e.*, investor does not materially participate in the activities of the investment) as a source of tax-sheltered income.

PIK **Payment In Kind**

Payment for goods and services with other goods and services rather than cash or securities; investments, bonds or preferred stock that pays interest or dividends in the form of additional bonds or shares of preferred stock.

P

PIL   **Payment In Lieu**

Payment for goods and services in cash or securities rather than goods or services as agreed upon.

PIMS   **Profit Impact Marketing Strategies**

A model for estimating the impact on profit from a change in the marketing mix.

PIN   **Personal Identification Number**

Number, generally selected by the customer, used to access funds or account information electronically.

PIP   **Payment In Part**

Indicator of partial payment of an invoice or other amount due.

Profit Improvement Program

Plan to increase the profitability of a product or service through a combination of maximizing sales or other revenue, and managing costs.

PIPS   **Paperless Item Processing System**

A business IT system that avoids the use of paper for processing payments etc.

PITI   **Principal, Interest, Taxes (property) and Insurance**

Real estate term for monthly payment required for a home mortgage loan.

PJ   **Purchases Journal**

Bookkeeping system in which all purchases are recorded before posting in the ledger.

P/L, P&L
     Profit and Loss

Summary of revenues, costs and expenses of a business entity during a financial reporting period.

PL   **Price List**

Reference summary of current prices charged for products and services, including information on discounts, etc.

P

PLN **Polish Zloty**

Currency of Poland

PMI **Private Mortgage Insurance**

Insurance on a conventional mortgage loan that indemnifies the lender from the borrower's default.

PO **Purchase Order**

Documentation between a customer and vendor setting forth the specifications of an order for goods, including terms of delivery and payment.

POP **Point of purchase**

A system that uses a computer terminal located at the point of sales transaction so that the data can be captured immediately by the computer system.

Proof of Posting

To prove by acceptable methods the accuracy of any posts made within ledgers or details confirming the shipment of mail with a postal office.

POS **Point-of-Sale**

The general point for revenue recognition. Generally accepted accounting principles (GAAP) require the recognition of revenue in the accounting period in which the sale is deemed to have occurred. For services, the sale is deemed to occur when the service is performed. In the case of merchandise, the sale takes place when the title to the goods transfers from seller to buyer. In many cases, this coincides with the delivery of the merchandise. As a result, accountants usually record revenue when goods are delivered.

PP **Pay Period**

Payroll management indicator of time period for which salaries and wages are paid.

Personal Property

Assets (tangible and intangible) other than real estate.

PPBS **Program-Planning-Budgeting System**

Planning-oriented approach to developing a budget in which expenditures are based primarily on programs of work and secondarily on character and object. The value of PPBS lies in the process of making program policy decisions that lead to a specific budget and plans for each year in which the program will run.

PPD **Pre-Paid**

Indicator that costs for goods or services purchased have been or must be paid before delivery.

PPI **Producer Price Index**

Measure of the cost of a given basket of goods priced in wholesale markets, including raw materials, semi-finished goods and finished goods, released monthly by the Bureau of Labor Statistics (U.S. Department of Commerce), signaling changes in the general price level or Consumer Price Index (CPI).

PPO **Preferred Provider Organizations**

A group of medical providers (doctors, hospitals, etc.) who contract with a health insurance company to provide services at a discount to policyholders if the policyholders choose to be served by PPO members.

PPP **Point-to-Point Protocol**

1. A protocol for communication between two computers, as opposed to a network.
2. A protocol that allows a computer to be its own Internet host.

PR **Payroll**

Records of employees to be paid and the amount due to each, the total of these amounts, funds to be paid out, and general processing and management involved in this function.

PRA **Prudential Regulation Authority**
(bankofengland.co.uk)

Is a part of the Bank of England and responsible for the prudential regulation and supervision of banks, building societies, credit unions, insurers and major investment firms. It sets standards and supervises financial institutions at the level of the individual firm

P

PRD **Payroll Deduction**

Withholding from salary and other compensation to provide for an individual's tax liability, employee benefits, etc.

PS **Profit Sharing**

Agreement between a corporation and its employees that allows employees to participate in the profits of the business.

PSBR **Public Sector Borrowing Requirement**

In the UK is the difference between tax receipts and total government spending. Public Sector Borrowing Requirement represents the annual fiscal deficit it has now been replaced by the Public Sector Net Cash Requirement.

PSDR **Public Sector Debt Requirement**

Forecast debt to be owed by the government at any level, such as local government or central government.

PSNCR **Public Sector Net Cash Requirement**

The Public Sector Net Cash Requirement was formerly known as the Public Sector Borrowing Requirement (PSBR). It represents the annual fiscal deficit (in cash terms).

PT **Payment**

Record-keeping indicator of an amount received corresponding with an amount owed.

Perfect Title

Generally referred to as Clear Title, indicating that title to a property is free of disputed interests.

Profit Taking

Cashing in short-term securities or commodities on gains earned in a sharp market rise.

Purchase Tax

British tax.

PTE **Pre-Tax Earnings**

Earnings or profits before federal income taxes.

PTY.LTD
Proprietary Limited

A term used in Australia, Singapore, and other countries for an owned corporation.

PUM   **Per Unit per Month.**

Refers to monthly revenue or expenses associated with each unit of production.

PV   **Present Value**

The value today of an amount to be received in the future based on an interest rate.

PVIF   **Present Value Interest Factor**

The projected future value of an investment of $1 discounted back to its present value. It is found in Table 3 (T3) in the Appendix.

PVIFA   **Present Value Interest Factor of an Annuity**

The total income stream of an annuity of $1 discounted to its present value. It is found in Table 4 (T4) in the Appendix.

PW   **Per Week**

Indicator of accounting of tabulating costs or other occurrences on a weekly basis.

PY   **Prior Year**

Refers to inclusion of financial information for the previous fiscal year or the same reporting period in the previous fiscal year, for comparison purposes.

PYR   **Prior Year Report**

Financial or other management reports for the previous fiscal year for comparison purposes.

P

Q

Q   **Quarter; Quarterly**

Occurring once every quarter year

QB   **Qualified Buyer**

Is a buyer of securities who is considered financially adept and is recognized by the regulators to need less protection than most public investors

QC   **Quality Control**

Any process a business uses to ensure that its product or service has a consistently high quality, using inspections, customer feedback and other tools at various points and times.

QE   **Quantitative Easing**

An extreme form of monetary policy used to stimulate an economy where interest rates have already been lowered to near 0% levels and have failed to produce the desired effect. The central bank uses an open market operation to increase the money supply by buying Treasury securities or other securities from the market. The major risk of this approach is that too much is chasing after a fixed amount of goods for sale, possibly leading to higher prices or inflation.

QOR   **Quarterly Operating Report**

Financial and other management information compiled every three months.

QP   **Quadratic Programming**

Special class of mathematical programming similar to linear programming, quadratic programming is most often and best applied to models directed at minimizing some measure of risk associated with a portfolio while maximizing return on the total investment, the objective being to determine the amount of funds to commit to each security from among a number of potential securities.

QPRT Qualified Personal Residence Trust

An estate-planning mechanism in which the owner of a personal residence (which can include a vacation home) transfers a remainder interest in the property to his descendants or other named beneficiaries, reserving a right to occupy and use the residence for a specified term. The present value of the reserved right, determined by application of government-provided factors, can be subtracted from the value of the property at the time of the gift in order derive the federal gift tax (FGT) value of the transfer. If the transferor dies before the term use interest expires, the value of the entire property at the transferor's death is taxed as part of the entire estate for federal estate tax (FET) purposes.

QQQ Nasdaq 100 Index Tracking Stock

An Exchange Traded Fund (ETF) which allows investors to basically invest in all of the stocks that compose the NASDAQ 100 in a single security.

QVEC Qualified Voluntary Employee Contribution

Generally ongoing employee-initiated payroll deductions to fund certain employee benefits, such as insurance coverage for dependents.

Q

R

(r) Correlation Coefficient

Measures the degree of correlation between two variables. The value range is between -1 and +1. A positive value shows a direct relationship; a negative value indicates an inverse relationship; a value of 0 indicates that the two variables are independent; a value of 1 shows that the two variables are perfectly correlated.

(r^2) Coefficient of Determination

Measures how good the estimated regression equation is – how good the fit is. The higher the r^2, the more confidence you should have on the estimated formula.

RA Restricted Account

Margin account with a securities broker in which the equity is less than the initial margin set by Federal Reserve Board regulations.

R&D Research and Development

Activity responsible for creating new products and doing the research for marketing and manufacturing needs.

RAM Random Access Memory

A computer's main memory where it can store data, so the size of the RAM (measured by kilobytes) is an important indicator of the capacity of the computer, also called read/write memory. RAM chips can be added to your computer to increase its memory. The characteristics of the RAM are:

1. Usable memory programmed into the computer by the user.

2. Where application software is being run.

3. Altered by user programs.

4. Easily accessed or altered.

5. Restricted capacity.

Reverse Annuity Mortgage

Mortgage loan that allows the homeowner-borrower (generally elderly) to live off of the substantial equity in the property.

RAR   Reserve/Asset Ratio

Ratio of cash reserves to total tangible assets.

RB   Revenue Bond

See MUNIS.

RC   Registered Check

Similar to a certified check, a check issued by a bank for a customer who places funds aside in a special account but does not have a regular checking account.

Replacement Cost

The cost to replace an asset or piece of property with another of similar utility at current prices.

RCA   Replacement Cost Accounting

Practice of valuing assets and property at replacement value.

RE   Reversing Entry

Accounting and bookkeeping notation that refers to a journal or ledger entry that generally corrects an entry previously made in error.

REDS   Refunding Escrow Deposits

Financial instruments that locks in a lower current rate in anticipation of maturing higher-rate issues by way of a forward purchase contract that obligates investors to buy bonds at a predetermined rate when they are issued at a future date that coincides with the first optional call date on existing high-rate bonds. In the interim, investors' money is invested in Treasury bonds, bought in the secondary market, which are held in escrow, effectively securing the investor's deposit and paying taxable annual income. The Treasuries mature around the call date on the existing bonds, thereby providing the money to buy the new issue and redeem the old one.

REG A Regulation A

A regulation under the Securities Act of 1933 providing for a simplified form of filing with the SEC, used for certain public offerings of not more than $5,000,000 and exempting such offerings from full registration.

R

REG D   Regulation D

A regulation under the Securities Act of 1933 which exempts limited offers and sales of securities from registration if the offering satisfies certain requirements as to the number and nature of investors and the value of the offering. Advertising and resale are restricted.

REG S   Regulation S

A regulation under the Securities Act of 1933 which exempts from registration certain offers and sales of securities made outside of the United States by USA or foreign issuers.

REIT   Real Estate Investment Trust

A type of investment company that invests money (obtained through the sale of its shares to investors) in mortgages and various types of investments in real estate, in order to earn profits for shareholders. The three types of REITs are:

1. Equity REITs: Invest primarily in income-producing properties.

2. Mortgage REITs: Lend funds to developers or builders.

3. Hybrid REITs: Combination of equity and mortgage REITs.

REIT Fact Book
Real Estate Investment Trust Fact Book

Annual publication published by the National Association of Real Estate Investment Trusts.

RELP   Real Estate Limited Partnership

Limited partnership that invests in real estate and passes rental and other income through to limited partners.

REMIC   Real Estate Mortgage Investment Conduit

Pass-through vehicle created in Tax Reform Act of 1986 for issuing multi-class mortgage-backed securities.

REO   Real Estate Owned

Real estate properties foreclosed upon or title otherwise reverting to a lending institution.

REPO   Repurchase Agreement

The temporary sale of securities (such as U.S. Treasury or government agency securities, bankers' acceptances, certificates of deposit, commercial paper and other marketable securities) to the investor (lender) accompanied by an agreement to repurchase them at some point in the near future. There is a provision for interest to be paid to the investor at the end of the transaction. Theoretically, the funds borrowed are collateralized by securities.

RERC **Real Estate Research Corporation**
(www.rerc.com)

Chicago-based organization that undertakes independent research projects on trends and opportunities within the real estate industry.

RFI **Request for Information**

A request to vendors for general, somewhat informal, information about their products.

RFP **Request for Proposal**

Process by which a customer procures proposals or bids for a service or product from one or more prospective vendors, setting forth the customer's specifications and expectations and asking that all proposals follow certain guidelines so the customer can make valid comparisons.

RHM **RHM Survey of Warrants, Options & Low-Priced Stock**

Weekly publication which provides investment advice on warrants, call and put options and low-priced stocks. Located in Glen Cove, NY.

RI **Residual Income**

The operating income which an investment center is able to earn above some minimum return on its assets. It is a popular alternative performance measure to return on investment (ROI). RI is computed as:

RI = Net operating income - (minimum rate of return on investment x operating assets).

Residual income, unlike ROI, is an absolute amount of income rather than a rate of return. When RI is used to evaluate divisional performance, the objective is to maximize the total amount of residual income, not to maximize the overall ROI percentage figure. For example, assume that operating assets is $100,000, net operating income is $18,000, and the minimum return on assets is 13 percent. Residual income is $18,000 - (13% x $100,000) =

R

$18,000 - $13,000 = $5,000. RI is sometimes preferred over ROI as a performance measure because it encourages managers to accept investment opportunities that have rates of return greater than the charge for invested capital. Managers being evaluated using ROI may be reluctant to accept new investments that lower their current ROI although the investments would be desirable for the entire company. Advantages of using residual income in evaluating divisional performance include:

1. it is an economic income taking into account the opportunity cost of tying up assets in the division;

2. the minimum rate of return can vary depending on the riskiness of the division;

3. different assets can be required to earn different returns depending on their risk;

4. the same asset may be required to earn the same return regardless of the division it is in; and

5. maximizing dollars rather than a percentage leads goal congruence.

RIA   **Research Institute of America**

(www.ria.thomsonreuters.com)

New York City-based publisher of a range of widely used business reference materials.

RICO   **Racketeer Influenced and Corrupt Organization Act**

Federal law used to prosecute firms and individuals of insider trading.

RIF   **Reduction in Force**

The formal term for downsizing, that is, when the company has reduced its workforce.

RMA   **Risk Management Association**

(www.rmahq.org)

A not-for-profit, member-driven professional association whose sole purpose is to advance the use of sound risk principles in the financial services industry. RMA helps banking and nonbanking institutions identify and manage the impacts of credit risk, operational risk, and market risk on their businesses and customers.

R

ROA   Return on Assets

Ratio that shows whether management is using resources efficiently to produce a profit. If the ratio decreases over time, that shows that the productivity of assets in generating earnings has deteriorated.

Formula:

$$\text{Return on Total Assets} = \frac{\text{Net Income}}{\text{Average Total Assets}}$$

ROC   Return on Capital

Distribution of cash resulting from depreciation tax savings, the sale of a capital asset or securities or any other transaction unrelated to retained earnings, also referred to as Return of Basis.

ROCE   Return on Capital Employed

Return on capital employed is an accounting ratio used in finance, valuation, and accounting.

ROE   Return on Equity

Earnings on a company's common stock investment for a given period, expressed as a percentage. The formula is:

$$\text{ROE} - \frac{\text{Net income available to stockholders}}{\text{Average stockholder's equity}}$$

ROI   Return on Investment

1. For the company as a whole, net income divided by invested capital. Invested capital may be total assets or stockholders' equity. Depending upon which is used as a measure of invested capital, there are two key ratios – the rate of return on total assets (ROA) and rate of return on stockholder's equity (ROE). For example, assume that net income is $18,000 and total assets are $100,000. The ROA is then $18,000/$100,000=18%. If the stockholder's equity is $90,000, the ROE would be $18,000/$90,000=20%.

2. For a segment of an organization, net operating income divided by operating assets.

3. For *capital budgeting* purposes, expected future net income divided by initial (or average) investment; also called *simple*, *accounting*, or *unadjusted rate of return*, *See also* **ARR**.

ROL **Reduction Option Loan**

Hybrid between fixed-rate and adjustable rate mortgage.

ROM **Read-Only Memory**

The memory that contains instructions that do not need to be altered. The computer can read instructions out of ROM, but no data can be stored in ROM. It is the permanent memory of the computer put in by the manufacturers that cannot be altered.

ROP **Reorder Point**

Also called Economic Order Point, establishes when to place a new order. Formula:

Reorder Point = Average usage per unit of lead time x lead time + Safety stock

Note

If average usage and lead time are both certain, then safety stock can be omitted from the formula.

Example

If lead time is 1 week, the year has 52 working weeks and average usage per unit of lead time is 150 (7,800 pieces/52 weeks), the reorder point 150.

ROS **Run on Schedule**

A product or service advertised on television or radio when it's suitable for programming. Usually means a lower rate.

Return on Sales

Net pretax profits as a percentage of net sales.

RP **Repurchase Agreement**

See REPO.

Reserve Purchase

Indicates a purchase, generally of a capital asset, being made from reserve funds as opposed to an operating budget.

RRM **Rate of Return Method**

General term to provide a category for a number of refined rate of return methods being used in analyzing investments.

Renegotiable Rate Mortgage or Renegotiated Rate Mortgage

Mortgage loan in which the lender requires the borrower to renegotiate and requalify at specified intervals during the term of the loan.

RRP   Recommended Retail Price.

Indicates a manufacturer's recommendation to retailers of pricing for a given item of merchandise.

RRR   Required Rate of Return

Indicates the minimum return an investor will accept in order to participate or invest.

RRSP   Registered Retirement Savings Plan

Tax-deductible and tax-sheltered retirement plan for Canadian taxpayers, similar to Individual Retirement Account (IRA) plans in the U.S.

RS   Revenue Sharing

Return of tax revenue to one unit of government by a larger unit, such as from a state to one of its municipalities. In investments, the percentage split between the general partner and limited partners of profits, losses, etc.

RUR   Russian Rouble

Currency of Russia

RWA   Returned without Action

An export license in international trade that is submitted because there is a missing or incorrect item. Once the correction is made, the application is resubmitted.

R

S

S   **Savings; Expenditure Saved**

Indicates an amount reserved for investment or budgeted for expenditure but not spent.

SA   **Savings Account**

Interest-earning deposit account at a commercial bank, savings bank, or savings and loan association.

S&D   **Special and Differential Treatment**

Special considerations given to the exports of developing countries to improve their economic and financial base. This may include lower or no tariffs and the easing of trade barriers.

SAIF   **Savings Association Insurance Fund**

U.S. Government entity created in 1989 to replace FSLIC as source of deposit insurance for thrift institutions.

S&L   **Savings and Loan Association**

Federally or state chartered depository financial institution that obtains the bulk of its deposits from consumers and holds the majority of its assets as home mortgage loans.

S&L, S/L
    Sale and Leaseback or Sale-Leaseback

Simultaneous purchase of real estate and lease back to the seller, generally on a long-term lease. The seller-lessee receives the proceeds of the sale while retaining occupancy of the property.

SALLIE MAE
    Student Loan Marketing Association Securities

Purchases by the Student Loan Marketing Association (Sallie Mae) of loans made by financial institutions under a variety of federal and state loan programs. Sallie Mae securities are not guaranteed, but are generally insured by the federal government and its agencies. These securities include floating rate and fixed rate obligations with maturities of five years or more as well as discount notes with maturities from a few days to 360 days.

SAM **Shared Appreciation Mortgage**

Mortgage loan involving two co-borrowers, generally one of whom occupies the property. Less frequently called a SEM – Shared Equity Mortgage, and informally called a CYD – "Call Your Dad" mortgage.

S&P **Standard and Poor's**

Company that provides a broad range of investment services, primarily rating bonds and stocks, and compiling indexes and publishing statistics, advisory reports and financial information.

S&P 500
Standard & Poor's 500 Stock Composite

The 500 Stock Composite Index calculated by Standard & Poor's. It differs from the Dow Jones Industrial Average (DJIA) in several important ways. First, it is a value-weighted, rather than price-weighted, index. This means that the index considers not only the price of a stock but also the number of shares outstanding. That is to say, it is based on the aggregate market value of the stock; i.e., price times number of shares. An advantage of the index over the DJIA is that stock splits and stock dividends do not affect the index value. A disadvantage is that large capitalization stocks –those with a large number of shares outstanding – heavily influence the index value. The S&P 500 actually consists of four separate indexes: the 400 industrials, the 40 utilities, the 20 transportation, and the 40 financial.

SAR **Semi-Annual Report**

Any financial or management report produced or published at the midpoint of the fiscal year.

Saudia Arabian Riyal

Currency of The Kingdom of Saudia Arabia

SAS **Statement on Auditing Standards**

Rule of auditing standards developed and issued by the Financial Accounting Standards Board.

SB **Statement of Billing**

Invoice for products or services sold.

S

Savings Bond

U.S. government bond issued at a discount of their face value and earning interest to and sometimes beyond maturity, the interest being exempt from state and load taxes, and sometimes from federal taxes.

SBA ### Small Business Administration
(www.sba.gov)

U.S. Government agency providing management and financial assistance to businesses that lack the resources to pursue capital and other advantages available to larger corporations. The SBA also has a 24-hour electronic bulletin board that provides information on SBA export and financial assistance, speakers, a women's mentor program, minority programs, and a mailbox for electronic discussions. The toll free numbers are: 1-800-859-4646 (2400 baud modem); 1-800-697-4636 (9600 baud modem).

SBLA ### Small Business Loans Act

Canadian legislation providing government funding for small business owners.

SBU ### Strategic Business Unit

A unit within an organization that sells a distinct set of products and services to an identified customer base in competition with well-defined competitors. These units operate within the objectives and strategies of top management. Within the framework, each SBU performs its own strategic management process. For example, SBUs of General Electric are aircraft engines, appliances, broadcasting, industrial, materials, power systems, technical, and capital services.

SC ### Service Charge

Designates an amount being billed to a customer or an account for a specific service being provided.

SCD ### Senior Citizen Discount

Designates a price reduction (generally a percentage) for customers over a certain age (generally 65).

SCM ### Supply Chain Management

Managing upstream and downstream value-added flows of materials, final goods, and related information among suppliers,

S

the company, resellers, and final consumers. It is a set of programs undertaken to increase the efficiency of distribution systems that moves products from the producer's facilities to the end user. By sharing information, production lead times and inventory holding costs have been reduced, while on-time deliveries to customers have been improved. SCM software systems support the planning of the best way to fill orders and help tracking of products and components among companies in the supply chain.

SCORE Service Corps of Retired Executives
(www.score.org)

National organization that matches retired executives offering their skills and experience with organizations that need short-term consulting and other services.

SD Safe Deposit

Bank service providing safekeeping for valuables, important documents, etc.

Sight Draft

Draft payable upon presentation by the designee.

Standard Deduction

An individual taxpayer's alternative to itemizing deductions on an income tax return.

Stock Dividend

Payment of a corporate dividend in the form of stock rather than cash.

SDFS Same-Day Funds Settlement

Method of settlement in good-the-same-day federal funds.

SDR Special Drawing Rights

An artificial official reserve asset held on the books of the International Monetary Fund (IMF). Unlike gold, SDRs have no tangible life of their own and take the form of bookkeeping entries in a special account managed by the Fund. They are used as the instruments for financing international trade.

S

SE **Self-Employed, Self-Employment**

Earning one's living directly from one's own profession or business, as opposed to as an employee earning salary, commissions or wages.

Shareholders' Equity; Stockholders' Equity

Total assets minus total liabilities: Net Worth.

Single-Entry Bookkeeping

Simple accounting system noting only amounts owed by and due to a business.

SEC **Securities and Exchange Commission**

(www.sec.gov)

A federal agency created by the Securities Exchange Act of 1934 to protect investors from dangerous or illegal financial practices or fraud by requiring full and accurate financial disclosure by companies offering stocks, bonds, mutual funds, and other securities to the public. It is the chief regulator of the U.S. securities market and overseer of the nation's stock exchanges, broker-dealers, investment advisors, and mutual funds.

SEEPAD
South Eastern European Partnership on Accountancy Development

A regional accountancy reform initiative consisting of the principle accounting and/or audit associations in South Eastern Europe.

SEI **Self-Employment Income**

Taxable income earned through self-employment as opposed or in addition to salary, wage and commission income from an employer.

SEK **Swedish Krona**

Currency of Sweden.

SEM **Shared-Equity Mortgage**

See SAM – Shared Appreciation Mortgage.

Strategic Enterprise Management

This is a method of management and the systems specifically

S

created to assist businesses when making high-level strategic decisions

SEP   Simplified Employee Pension

Pension plan in which both the employee and employer contribute to the employee's Individual Retirement Account (IRA), with tax benefits and compliance requirements for both employee and employer.

SERP   Self-Employed Retirement Plan

Tax-deferred pension plan for self-employed individuals and employees of small, unincorporated businesses, also called Keogh Plan.

SF   Sinking Fund

Money accumulated on a regular basis in a separate custodial account that is used to extinguish an indebtedness, usually a bond issue.

SFAC   Statements of Financial Accounting Concepts

Concepts statements that guide the Board in developing sound accounting principles and provide the Board and its constituents with an understanding of the appropriate content and inherent limitations of financial reporting. SFAC does not establish generally accepted accounting standards.

SFAS   Statement of Financial Accounting Standards

Rule of accounting practice developed and issued by the Financial Accounting Standards Board (FASB).

SG&A   Sales, General and Administrative Expenses

The costs contained within the Sales, General and Administrative expense/cost categories.

SGD   Signed

An acronym for "signed."

Singapore Dollar

Currency of Singapore

S

SGR **Sustainable Growth Rate**

The rate at which a company can grow using internally generated assets without issuing additional debt or equity. SGR provides a useful benchmark for judging a company's appropriate rate of growth. A company with a low SGR but lots of opportunities for expansion will have to fund that growth using outside financing sources, which could lower profits and perhaps strain the company's finances.

SH **Stockholder or Shareholder**

Individual or organization with an ownership position in a corporation.

SHRM **Society for Human Resource Management**
(www.shrm.org)

The world's largest association devoted to human resource management. Representing more than 250,000 members in over 140 countries, the Society serves the needs of HR professionals and advances the interests of the HR profession. Founded in 1948, SHRM has more than 575 affiliated chapters within the United States and subsidiary offices in China and India.

SI **Simple Interest**

Calculation of interest based only on the original principal amount, rather than interest compounding over the term of the loan.

SIA **Securities Industry Association**

U.S. trade group representing securities broker-dealers.

SIC **Standard Industrial Classification System**

A digital coding system that classifies industry types and firms into groups and subgroups. The SIC classifies business firms by the main product or service provided. Firms are classified into one of ten basic SIC industries. Within each classification, the major groups of industries can be identified by the first two numbers of the SIC code. For example, SIC number 22 are textile mills, SIC number 34 are manufacturers of fabricated metals, and so on. An industrial producer would attempt to identify the manufacturing groups that represent potential users of the products it produces and sells. Exhibit 1 takes the two-digit classification and converts it to three-, four-, five-, and seven-digit codes. Use of the SIC code

S

allows the industrial manufacturer to identify the organizations whose principal request is, in this case, pliers. Based upon this list of construction machinery and equipment products, it is possible to determine what products are produced by what manufacturers by consulting one of the following sources:

- Dun's Market Identifiers—computer-based records of three minion United States and Canadian business establishments by four-digit SIC.

- Metalworking Directory—a comprehensive list of metalworking plants with 20 or more employees, as well as metal distributors, by four-digit SIC.

- Thomas Register of American Manufacturers—a directory of manufacturers, classified by products, enabling the researcher to identify most or all of the manufacturers of any given product.

- Survey of Industrial Purchasing Power—an annual survey of manufacturing activity in the United States by geographic areas and four-digit SIC industry groups; reports the number of plants with 20 or more and 100 or more employees, as well as total shipment value.

Exhibit 1: SIC two-digit to seven-digit classification

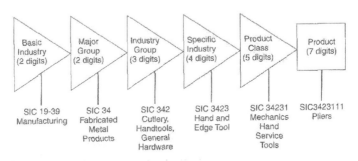

Basic Industry (2 digits)	Major Group (2 digits)	Industry Group (3 digits)	Specific Industry (4 digits)	Product Class (5 digits)	Product (7 digits)
SIC 19-39 Manufacturing	SIC 34 Fabricated Metal Products	SIC 342 Cutlery, Handtools, General Hardware	SIC 3423 Hand and Edge Tool	SIC 34231 Mechanics Hand Service Tools	SIC3423111 Pliers

SIMPLE Savings Incentive Match Plan for Employees

Retirement plan created by the Taxpayer Relief Act of 1997.

SIPC   Securities Investor Protection Corporation
(www.sipc.org)

Nonprofit organization established by Congress that insures securities and cash in customer accounts of member brokerage firms

S

SIOR   **Society of Industrial and Office Realtors**
(www.sior.com)

Washington, D.C.-based trade organization, affiliated with the National Association of Realtors.

SKU   **Stock Keeping Unit**

A specific item that a reseller stocks (for example, a 5,000-watt Dayton professional duty, portable, gasoline power generator is an SKU).

It refers to a specific identifying stock number for each separate product carried out by store.

S/M; S&M
   Service/Maintenance or Service and Maintenance

Designates an income or expense category for service and maintenance of equipment, facilities, etc.

SMA   **Separately Managed Accounts**

Managed accounts with customized investment products in search of a performance edge or just the ability to brag about having a personal money manager. The allure of SMAs stems from their flexibility and transparency. Don't like semiconductor stocks? No problem. Your religious beliefs ban owning "sin stocks"? They're out. As for transparency, you get a list of this week's trades, the website address and the password so you can check up on your holdings. SMAs can be pricy, especially for smaller investors. While US stock mutual funds charge an average of 1.4 percent in fees, SMA fees can top 3 percent. There is disagreement on the point at which they become "fee-efficient".

SML   **Security Market Line**

This line graph shows the relationship between risk as measure by beta and the required rate of return for individual securities. The equation (See Exhibit 1), is given as follows: $r_i = r_f + b (r_m - r_f)$ where r_i = the expected (or required) return on security I, r_f = the risk-free security (such as a T-bill), r_m = the expected return on the market portfolio (such as Standard & Poor's 500 Stock Composite Index), and b = Beta, an index of non-diversifiable (noncontrollable, systematic) risk. In words, the CAPM or (SML) equation shows that the required (expected) rate of return on a given security (r_i) is equal to the return required for securities that have no risk (r_f) plus a risk premium required by investors for

S

assuming a given level of risk. The higher the degree of systematic risk (b), the higher the return on a given security demanded by investors.

Exhibit 1: Security Market Line

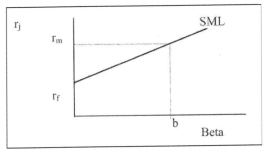

SMSA   Standard Metropolitan Statistical Area

Socioeconomic census areas defined by population and economic-geographic characteristics. This designation by the U.S. Census Bureau of a geographic area is helpful to businesses particularly for advertising.

SO   Sales Order or Stock Order

Documentation or record-keeping system, usually numbered serially, of orders placed and processed.

SOHO   Small Office/Home Office

The fastest growing type of business, thanks to the availability of inexpensive information technology, such as PCs and fax/modems; also called TOHO (Tiny Office/Home office).

SOP   Standard of Practice

One of a series of guidelines published by the AICPA to assist practitioners in adhering to high standards of ethics and consistency in completing engagements.

Standard Operating Procedure or Standard Operating Plan

An organization's official statement of its routine or expected method for executing a specific task or responding to a certain situation.

S

SORPS **Statement of Recommended Practice**

Are sector-driven recommendations on accounting practices for specialised industries or sectors which supplement accounting standards

SOX **Sarbanes-Oxley Act**

Wide-ranging U.S. corporate reform legislation, coauthored by the Democrat in charge of the Senate Banking Committee, Paul Sarbanes, and Republican Congressman Michael Oxley. The Act, which became law in July 2002, lays down stringent procedures regarding the accuracy and reliability of corporate disclosures, places restrictions on auditors providing non-audit services and obliges top executives to verify their accounts personally. Section 409 is especially tough and requires that companies must disclose information on material changes in the financial condition or operations of the issuer on a rapid and current basis.

SOYD **Sum-of-The-Year's-Digits Depreciation**

See *SYD*.

SP **Stop Payment**

Revocation of payment on a written check after the check has been sent or delivered to a payee.

SPA **Societe per Azionie**

An Italian term for public corporation. The corporation must have at least two shareholders at formation.

SPDA **Single-Premium Deferred Annuity**

Tax-deferred investment similar to an Individual Retirement Account but without many of an IRA's restrictions.

SPDR **Standard & Poor's Depositary Receipt**

Shares of a security designed to track the value of the S&P 500; also called *SPDRs* or *Spiders*. Spiders trade on the American Stock Exchange under the symbol SPY. One SPDR unit is valued at approximately one-tenth of the value of the S&P 500. Dividends are distributed quarterly, and are based on the accumulated stock dividends held in trust, less any expenses of the trust.

SPE **Special Purpose Entity**

A type of corporate entity or limited partnership created for a specific transaction or business, especially one unrelated to a company's main business; also called *special purpose vehicle (SPV)*. Their losses and risks generally aren't recorded on a company's balance sheet. This is a separate company, usually established as a charitable trust, set up to take legal rights over assets sold to it by the parent company.

SPV   Special Purpose Vehicle

See SPE.

SPWL   Single-Premium Whole Life (Insurance)

Low-risk investment life insurance policy in which for a one-time payment of a minimum amount, the policyholder receives a paid-up insurance policy. The money is invested at a guaranteed rate of interest for one year or longer.

Features of SPWL:

1. The cash value earns interest at competitive rates from the date of the policy.

2. The policyholder can borrow interest earned annually after the first year.

3. The policyholder can take out a low-interest loan for 90% of the principal.

4. The policyholder receives permanent life insurance coverage.

5. Withdrawals and loans before age 59-1/2 are subject to a nondeductible tax penalty.

6. Cash value accumulates tax-deferred.

7. Death benefits are paid to beneficiaries tax-free.

Significant disadvantages:

1. Surrender charges are generally incurred if the money is taken out.

2. The interest rate is generally guaranteed for only one year, and can decrease.

SQC   Smaller Quoted Companies

SREA   Senior Real Estate Analyst

Professional certification offered by the Society of Real Estate Appraisers

S

SRO **Self-Regulatory Organization**

Any organization formed by various parties within a trade or industry to provide governance and oversight independent of government controls.

SRP **Salary Reduction Plan**

Employee benefit program that allows employees contribute compensation to qualified retirement or other benefit plan on a pretax basis.

SS **Social Security**

Aggregate taxpayer benefits under the Social Security Act of 1935.

SSA **Social Security Administration**

(www.ssa.gov)

U.S. Government agency responsible for maintaining and administering the Social Security program.

SSAPs **Statements of Standard Accounting Practices**

Accounting standards to be followed by UK accountants to try and ensure consistent and effective measurement and presentation of financial statements. They are linked to but not identical to Generally Accepted Accounting Practices (GAAP) . These may in turn differ from country to country (i.e. Germany and USA).

To an extent the introduction of International Financial Reporting Standard (IFRS) are attempting to harmonise standards internationally.

There are at least 8 SSAPs applied now: Government grants, Value Added Tax (VAT), Stock and long term contracts, Research and Development (R & D), investment properties, foreign currency , leases and hire purchase contracts, segmental reporting.

ST **Sales Tax**

State and/or local government tax based on a percentage of the selling price of goods and services.

STL **Short-Term Loan**

Loan expected to be repaid within one year.

S

STAGS Sterling Transferable Accruing Government Securities

British bonds backed by British Treasury securities.

S/V Surrender Value

Amount of money an insurer will return to a policyholder upon cancellation of a policy.

SWIFT Society for Worldwide Interbank Financial Telecommunications

(www.swift.com)

A worldwide dedicated computer network that provides funds transfer messages between member banks.

SWOT Strengths (S), Weaknesses (W), Opportunities (O), And Threats (T)

Analysis of a company's strengths (S) and weaknesses (W) in light of the threats (T) and opportunities (O) presented by the environment. A SWOT analysis stresses that the organizational strategies must result in a proper fit between the organization's internal and external environments. For example, as the usage of the Internet and electronic commerce continues to rise, a software company tries to extend its exploitation of this market by acquiring and merging with companies with specialized Web expertise, such as an Internet service provider, makers of a Web page creation system, makers, of object-oriented programming software, and makers of Internet commerce software

SYD Sum-of-The-Year's-Digits Depreciation

An accelerated depreciation method where the amounts recognized in the early periods of an asset's useful life are greater than those recognized in the later periods. That fraction is formed with the numerator being the year in question and the denominator being the sum of the asset's years of useful life. Sometimes referred to as SOYD.

S

T

TA   **Tangible Asset**

Any asset other than a nonphysical right to something presumed to represent an advantage in the marketplace, such as goodwill, patents and trademarks.

T/A   **Trade Acceptance**

A time draft or date draft similar to a banker's acceptance, the difference being that a bank is not a party. The exporter presents the draft to the importer (the buyer or drawee) for its acceptance to pay the amount stated at maturity. Trade acceptances cannot become bankers' acceptances or be guaranteed by a United States bank.

TAA   **Trade Adjustment Assistance**

The TAA is a United States policy authorized by the 1974 Trade Act to offer aid to workers laid off due to competition from imported goods. Such assistance includes job placement, instruction, and relocation support.

TAB   **Tax Anticipation Bill**

Short-term obligation issued by the U.S. Treasury.

T&B   **Time and Billing (Software)**

Computer software that tracks hours incurred by activity for different staff for a particular client or project. Sources of time information include hourly rates, time sheets, practice management reports, and financial reports. At the end of each period, a bill is prepared based on hours worked and billing rates for each individual reporting time for each client and/or project.

TAC   **Total Annualized Cost**

Projected expense in a given category over a 12-month period.

T&E   **Travel and Entertainment**

Account for tracking and reimbursing travel and entertainment expenses.

TALP **Term Asset-Backed Loan Facility Program**

A program created by the U.S. Federal Reserve Board, announced on November 25, 2008. The facility will support the issuance of asset-backed securities (ABS) collateralized by student loans, auto loans, credit card loans, and loans guaranteed by the Small Business Administration (SBA). Under the TALF, the Federal Reserve Bank of New York (FRBNY) will lend up to $1 trillion on a non-recourse basis to holders of certain AAA-rated ABS backed by newly and recently originated consumer and small business loans.

TAM **Tax Advisory Memoranda**

Significant statements of position and interpretation on the Internal Revenue Code that are issued as needed by Treasury Department.

TAN **Tax Anticipation Note**

Short-term obligation of a state or municipal government to finance current expenditures pending receipt of expected tax payments.

TAP **Total Annualized Profit**

Projected revenue less expense in a given category over a 12-month period.

TARP **Troubled Asset Relief Program**

A program of the U.S government to purchase assets and equity from financial institutions in order to strengthen its financial sector. It is the largest component of the government's measures to curb the ongoing financial and subprime mortgage crisis of 2007-2008.

TB **Terabyte**

A trillion bytes, or a thousand Gigabyte (GB).

TBE **Tenancy by the Entirety**

Individual co-ownership that passes automatically upon the death of one co-owner to the surviving co-owner.

T.C. **Tax Court**

U.S. federal tax court.

T

TCP/IP **Transfer Control Protocol/Internet Protocol**

Protocol explaining the subdivision of information into packets for transmission, and the way in which applications involve transmitting e-mail and file transfer.

TD **Time Draft**

Draft payable at a specified date in the future, as opposed from a Sight Draft, which is payable upon presentation.

TDA **Tax Deferred Annuities**

A defined contribution plan available to teachers, hospitals, and nonprofit organizations; also called the *403(b) plan*.

TDAIR **Taxpayer Delinquent Account Information Record**

IRS recordkeeping mechanism.

TDI **Taxpayer Delinquent Investigation**

IRS term for routine follow up on past-due tax and/or penalty matters.

TE **Total Expenditure**

Sum of all expenses in a given category.

TEFRA **Tax Equity and Fiscal Responsibility Act**

Federal legislation of 1982.

10-K **Annual 10-K Report**

Contains the same the same type of information as a company's annual report, but in greater detail. It is the most widely known and can be obtained free directly from the company or from the SEC for a copying charge.

10-Q **Quarterly 10-Q Report**

A report filed by a corporation when it experiences an important event that stockholders would be interested in knowing about. Such changes include bankruptcy, change in control and officer or director resignations.

THLRA **Taft-Hartley Labor Relations Act**

Also known as Labor Management Relations Act, passed into law in 1947, provisions of which include injunctions against labor strikes.

3G   Third Generation

Third-generation mobile technology that usually includes services such as video telephony, downloading information, e-mail, and instant messaging.

TI   Taxable Income

Income or revenue subject to local, state or federal income tax.

TIC   Tenancy in Common

Ownership of real estate by two or more individuals, in which ownership at the death of one co-owner is part of the co-owner's disposable estate.

TIF   Taxpayer Information File

IRS term for recordkeeping mechanism.

TIGER   Treasury Investors Growth Receipt

U.S. government-backed bonds that are sold at deep discounts to investors, who receive no periodic investors but receive full face value at maturity.

TILA   Truth in Lending Act

A major federal law designed to protect credit purchasers; also called, *Consumer Credit Protection Act of 1969; Regulation Z*. The most important provision is the requirement that both the dollar amount of finance charges and the annual percentage rate (APR) charged must be disclosed before credit is extended.

TIN   Taxpayer Identification Number

Usually the same as your Social Security number.

TIPS   Treasury Inflation-Protected Securities

Securities which are identical to treasury bonds except that principal and coupon payments are adjusted to eliminate the effects of inflation.

TIRA   Thrift Industry Recovery Act

Federal legislation enacted in 1987.

T

TL   **Total Loss**

Asset or property holding no present or future value because of damage, market reversal, etc.

TLI   **Term Life Insurance**

Life insurance policy written for a specific time period and paying the beneficiaries only in the event of the insured's death.

TMWR **Tax Management Weekly Report**

Reference publication from Bureau of National Affairs (BNA).

TO   **Treasury Obligation**

Any negotiable U.S. Treasury debt obligation.

TOC   **Theory of Constraints**

A manufacturing strategy that attempts to remove the influence of bottlenecks (constraints) on a process. A binding constraint can limit a company's profitability. For example, a manufacturing company may have a *bottleneck operation*, through which every unit of a product must pass before moving on to other operations. The TOC calls for identifying such limiting constraints and seeking ways to relax them. Also referred to as *managing constraints*, this management approach can significantly improve an organization's level of goal attainment. Among the ways that management can relax a constraint by expanding the capacity of a bottleneck operation are the following:

- *Outsourcing* (subcontracting) all or part of the bottle neck operation.

- Investing in additional production equipment and employing *parallel processing*, in which multiple product units undergo the same production operation simultaneously.

- Working *overtime* at the bottleneck operation.

- *Retaining* employees and shifting them to the bottleneck.

- Eliminating any *non-value-added activities* at the bottleneck operation.

TP   **Taxpayer**

Any person who pays a tax or is subject to taxation.

TPR **Temporary Price Reduction**

Short-term lowering of retail or whole sale price on a given product or service.

TPT **Third-Party Transaction**

Business agreement executed through a bank or other third party.

TQM **Total Quality Management**

An approach to quality that emphasizes continuous improvement, a philosophy of "doing it right the first time," and striving for zero defects and elimination of all waste. It is a concept of using quality methods and techniques to strategic advantage within firms. TQM is a system for creating competitive advantage by focusing the organization on what is important to the customer. Total quality management can be broken down into: "Total": that is the whole organization is involved and understands that customer satisfaction is everyone's job. "Quality": the extent to which products and services satisfy the requirements of internal and external customers. "Management": the leadership, infrastructure and resources that support employees as they meet the needs of those customers.

See also **BPR**.

TR **Tax Rate**

Percentage of tax to be paid on a certain level of income.

TRA **Tax Reform Act**

Major federal legislation enacting provisions affecting taxation.

TRSA **Tax Reduction and Simplification Act**

Federal legislation enacted in 1977

TS **Tax Shelter**

Mechanism used by an investor to legally avoid or reduce tax liabilities.

Treasury Stock

Nonvoting stock created by a company to accomplish specific objectives and which does not pay or accrue dividends.

T

TSA Tax-Sheltered Annuity

An employee-benefit plan similar to a 401(k) plan but available to employees of nonprofit organizations that are ineligible for a 401(k). With a TSA, an employee can withdraw funds at any age for any reason without tax penalty, and must pay ordinary taxes on all withdrawals.

TSOP Time Share Ownership Plan

Mechanism in which multiple owners of a piece of real estate (*e.g.*, vacation home) purchase a specific block of time for use of the property each year.

TTA Total Tax Expenditures

Sum of all taxes paid during a given accounting or financial reporting period.

12b-1 12b-1 Plans

Mutual fund fees that cover the cost of advertising and marketing. The main purpose of 12b-1 plans is to bring in new customers and, thus, more money for the fund to invest. The actual cost to the fund of a 12b-1 plan are listed in the front of the prospectus in the fee table.

T

U

UB   **Unemployment Benefits**

Payments made from federal and state unemployment insurance systems to laid-off workers, funded by a payroll tax on employers.

UBIT   **Unrelated Business Income Tax**

Tax on income to nonprofit organizations that is unrelated to the purpose for which the organization holds tax-exempt status.

UBTI   **Unrelated Business Taxable Income**

Income to a nonprofit organization that is taxable as being unrelated to the reason for which the organization holds tax-exempt status.

UCC   **Uniform Commercial Code**

The code that standardizes business law in this country. The Code was formulated in 1952 by the National Conference of Commissioners on United State Laws. The Code was offered to the state legislatures, and all states except Louisiana adopted it. For example, the Code covers regulations on commercial paper, warranties, uncertified checks, written agency agreements, security agreements, and bankruptcy. The Uniform Commercial Code is followed by practicing lawyers.

UGMA   **Uniform Gifts to Minors Act**

A uniform act establishing rules for transferring and administering assets to a minor. A custodian is designated to act on the behalf of the minor, making all related investment decisions, including buying and selling assets for the minor. All earned income is taxed to the minor. The custodianship ends when the child reaches the age of majority.

UIT   **Unit Investment Trust**

Investment comprising portfolios of fixed-income securities.

UKPS   **UK Payments Administration.**

UK Payments Administration Ltd is a service company providing people, facilities and expertise to the UK payments industry.

UN   Unrealized Loss

Loss that will not become actual until the security or property involved is sold, also called a paper loss.

UOT   Unit of Trading

Normal number of shares, bonds or commodities that make up the minimum unit of trading on an exchange

UP   Unrealized Profit

Profit that will not become actual until the security or property involved is sold, also called a paper profit.

UPC   Universal Product Code

System for assigning a unique bar code to a product or type of property, read using special scanning equipment and used for inventory and other management purposes.

UPD   Unpaid

Indicates an amount due or invoice not paid in full.

UPT   Undistributed Profits Tax

Surtax on earnings retained in a business to avoid higher personal income taxes, also called Accumulated Profits Tax and Accumulated Earnings Tax.

URL   Uniform Resource Locator

An address system used for the Internet. The http prefix is used for the WWW. For example,

http://www.amazon.com

is the full address for the Amazon online retail store.

Some common addresses

http://	World Wide Web
ftp://	FTP server
Gopher://	Gopher server
mailto://	e-mail
news://	Newsgroup
wais://	Wide Area Information Server

U

USCC **United States Chamber of Commerce**
(www.uschamber.com)
The world's largest business federation representing the interests of more than 3 million businesses of all sizes, sectors, and regions, as well as state and local chambers and industry associations. More than 96% of U.S. Chamber members are small businesses with 100 employees or fewer.

USD **United States Dollar**
Currency of the United States of America

USIT **Unit Share Investment Trust**
Special type of Unit Investment Trust.

USLSI **United States League of Savings Institutions**
National trade organization.

USP **Unique Selling Point**
Is something that sets a business, product, or service apart from the competition.

VA Veterans Administration

(www.va.gov)

A federal government agency that helps veterans of the armed forces obtain housing. For example, it guarantees a home loan for up to a specified dollar amount or percentage of the loan balance, whichever is less.

V/A Value Added

Concept of building additional benefits into a product or service to make it more attractive to prospective customers and to retain existing customers.

VAT Value Added Tax

An indirect percentage tax levied on products or services at various stages of production and distribution. The actual value added to the product, including raw materials, labor and profit, is determined at each stage or state of production and the tax is computed upon the increase in value. It is basically a tax allocated among the economic units responsible for the production and distribution of goods and services. Collection of VAT takes place at the product's ultimate destination, therefore VAT is not charged on export sales. VAT is charged on all domestically sold products regardless of the country of origin. Thus, VAT is designed to provide an incentive to export and of course a disincentive to import.

VBM Value Based Management

A management approach that ensures businesses are run continuously on value

VC Variable Costs

Cost that vary with a measure of activity. Examples are direct materials, direct labor, and sale commissions.

Venture Capital

Source of financing for start-up companies and businesses undertaking major new developments.

VELDA SUE
Venture Enhancement and Loan Development Administration for Smaller Undercapitalized Enterprises

A federal agency that buys and pools small business loans made by banks, and then issues securities that are bought by large institutional investors.

VFD   Value for Duty

Worth of goods on which tariff for importation, exportation or consumption is charged.

VIR   Variable Interest Rate

Interest rate that rises or falls based on changes in interest rates in an index of interest rates.

VIX   Chicago Board Options Exchange Volatility Index

A popular measure of the implied volatility of S&P 500 index options; often called the *fear index*. The index represents one measure of the market's expectation of volatility over the next 30 day period. A high value corresponds to a more volatile market and therefore more costly options, which can be used to defray risk from volatility. If investors see high risks of a change in prices, they require a greater premium to insure against such a change by selling options.

VLI   Variable Life Insurance

Insurance policy in which the cash value of the policy is invested in stock, bond or money market portfolios.

VMS   Vertical Marketing System

A distribution channel structure in which producers, wholesalers, and retailers act as a unified system. One channel member owns the others, has contracts with them, or has so much power that they all cooperate.

VND   Vietnamese Dong

Currency of Vietnam

VPA   Volume Purchase Agreement

Contract for purchasing a large quantity of a given product, generally at a significant discount based on the quantity.

VRDB **Variable Rated Demand Bond**

Floating-rate bond that periodically can be sold back to the issuer.

VRM **Variable Rate Mortgage**

Similar to **ARM** (Adjustable Rate Mortgage), mortgage made at an interest rate that fluctuates depending on a base interest rate, such as the prime rate or LIBOR.

WACC Weighted Average Cost of Capital

Rate of return an investor could expect in another investment with equivalent risk. Each source of capital, such as stocks, bonds, and other debt, is weighted in the calculation according to its prominence in the company's capital structure.

WAN Wide Area Network

Network comprising of a large geographic area. The connected LANs to derive a WAN may be in the same building, or different buildings near each other or distantly apart. WANs are essential in the client/server environment because the applications in client/server usually apply to accessing data stored in separate locations.

WATS Wide Area Telephone Service

Lower-rate long distance telephone lines used by businesses.

WC Working Capital

Current assets minus current liabilities.

WCRI Workers Compensation Research Institute
(www.wcrinet.org)

Cambridge, Mass.-based organization providing research and other information resources on workers compensation insurance rates and rules.

WDV Written Down Value

Downward adjustment of the value of an asset according to Generally Accepted Accounting Principles (GAAP).

WH Withholding

Deduction from salary or other compensation or distributions for tax liabilities.

Work Hour(s)

Unit of timekeeping as tracked for billing or paying wages for work provided.

wi　　**When, as, and if issued**

Indicates that, if a stock is trading before it has cleared all legal requirements for issuance, all trades will be cancelled should the stock not be issued.

Wi-Fi　**Wireless Fidelity**

The popular term for a high-frequency wireless local area network. The consumer-friendly name for the 802.11b engineering standard. It lets home and office users create wireless local networks, which connect two or more computers to each other and a faster Internet line. This way there is no more poking holes in walls or tripping over bulky Ethernet cables. The Wi-Fi technology is rapidly gaining acceptance in many companies as an alternative to a wired local area network. It can also be installed for a home network.

WIP　　**Work-in-progress inventory**

Inventory of goods that are started but not finished. That is, partially completed units, not ready for sale.

WIPO　**World Intellectual Property Organization**

An international organization focused on the protection of intellectual property. WIPO administers 23 international treaties and is one of 16 specialized agencies of the United Nations. 183 nations are part of the WIPO and its headquarters is in Geneva, Switzerland.

WLAN　**Wireless Lan**

One in which a mobile user can connect to a local area network (Lan) through a wireless (radio) connection. A standard, 802.11 specifies the technologies for wireless Lans.

W/O　　**Write-Off**

To permanently charge an asset to expense or loss as a means of resolving an uncollectable or irretrievably depreciated item.

WOM　**Word-of-Mouth Advertising**

Advertising that occurs when people share information about products or promotions with friends. It is informal communications between consumers about products and services they like or dislike.

WPT   Windfall Profit Tax

Tax on profits resulting from a sudden event favorable to a particular company or industry.

WTO   World Trade Organization
(www.wto.org)

A permanent institution that sets rules governing trade between its members through a panel of trade experts who

1. decide on trade disputes between members and

2. issue binding decisions.

Ww   With warrants

Indicates that new issues of stock appear in units that include a number of warrants that may be detached and traded separately or remain with the stock certificates as specified. A warrant is an option that gives its holder the right to buy a security at a set price, either within a specified period of time or perpetually.

WYSIWYG
What you see is what you get

XBRL   Extensible Business Reporting Language

Formerly code named XFRML, a freely available electronic language for financial reporting. It is an XML-based framework that provides the financial community a standards-based method to prepare, publish in a variety of formats, reliably extract and automatically exchange financial statements of publicly held companies and the information they contain.

XML   Extensible Mark up Language

Is a markup language that defines a set of rules for encoding documents in a format that is both human-readable and machine-readable

Y

YS   **Yield Spread**

The difference between the yields received on two different types of bonds with different ratings.

YTD   **Year-to-Date**

Indicates that financial or other information shown reflects all occurrences in the current fiscal year through the present date.

YTM   **Yield to Maturity**

Fully compounded rate of return on a bond, assuming the bond is held to maturity. The formula for estimating YTM on a bond issued at a discount is:

$$\frac{\text{Stated Amount of Interest} + \dfrac{\text{Discount}}{\text{Years to Maturity}}}{\dfrac{\text{Current Price of Bond} - \text{Maturity Value}}{2}}$$

The formula for computing an estimate of the YTM when a bond is issues at a premium is:

$$\frac{\text{Stated Amount of Interest} + \dfrac{\text{Premium}}{\text{Years to Maturity}}}{\dfrac{\text{Current Price of Bond} - \text{Maturity Value}}{2}}$$

Z

ZAR **South African Rand**

Currency of South Africa

ZBA **Zero-Bracket Amount**

An arrangement, agreed to in advance by a drawee bank, under which a customer issues checks on an account even though funds do not exist in that account to cover the items. When the checks are physically presented to the drawee and posted, creating a minus balance, the bank contacts the customer, reports the overdraft figure, and transfers funds from another account to eliminate it, thus restoring the account to a zero balance. Commonly used by corporations that have many disbursing points and by many agencies of government.

ZBB **Zero-Based Budgeting**

Method of developing budgets that requires re-examination of all assumptions for both revenue and expenses, rather than adjustments to prior years' budgets or actual results. The basic steps are:

1. Determine objectives and activities required.

2. Evaluate alternative ways of accomplishing each activity.

3. Develop and review alternative budget figures for various possible future occurrences.

4. Formulate measurements for performance.

5, Rank activities in order of their importance to the organization.

Z

Appendix

TABLE 1: FUTURE VALUE OF $1 = FVIF = T1

Periods	4%	6%	8%	10%	12%	14%	20%
1	1.040	1.060	1.080	1.100	1.120	1.140	1.200
2	1.082	1.124	1.166	1.210	1.254	1.300	1.440
3	1.125	1.191	1.260	1.331	1.405	1.482	1.728
4	1.170	1.263	1.361	1.464	1.574	1.689	2.074
5	1.217	1.338	1.469	1.611	1.762	1.925	2.488
6	1.265	1.419	1.587	1.772	1.974	2.195	2.986
7	1.316	1.504	1.714	1.949	2.211	2.502	3.583
8	1.369	1.594	1.851	2.144	2.476	2.853	4.300
9	1.423	1.690	1.999	2.359	2.773	3.252	5.160
10	1.480	1.791	2.159	2.594	3.106	3.707	6.192
11	1.540	1.898	2.332	2.853	3.479	4.226	7.430
12	1.601	2.012	2.518	3.139	3.896	4.818	8.916
13	1.665	2.133	2.720	3.452	4.364	5.492	10.699
14	1.732	2.261	2.937	3.798	4.887	6.261	12.839
15	1.801	2.397	3.172	4.177	5.474	7.138	15.407
16	1.873	2.540	3.426	4.595	6.130	8.137	18.488
17	1.948	2.693	3.700	5.055	6.866	9.277	22.186
18	2.026	2.854	3.996	5.560	7.690	10.575	26.623
19	2.107	3.026	4.316	6.116	8.613	12.056	31.948
20	2.191	3.207	4.661	6.728	9.646	13.743	38.338
30	3.243	5.744	10.063	17.450	29.960	50.950	237.380
40	4.801	10.286	21.725	45.260	93.051	188.880	1469.800

TABLE 2: FUTURE VALUE OF AN ANNUITY OF $1 = FVIFA = T2

Periods	4%	6%	8%	10%	12%	14%	20%
1	1.000	1.000	1.000	1.000	1.000	1.000	1.000
2	2.040	2.060	2.080	2.100	2.120	2.140	2.200
3	3.122	3.184	3.246	3.310	3.374	3.440	3.640
4	4.247	4.375	4.506	4.641	4.779	4.921	5.368
5	5.416	5.637	5.867	6.105	6.353	6.610	7.442
6	6.633	6.975	7.336	7.716	8.115	8.536	9.930
7	7.898	8.394	8.923	9.487	10.089	10.730	12.916
8	9.214	9.898	10.637	11.436	12.300	13.233	16.499
9	10.583	11.491	12.488	13.580	14.776	16.085	20.799
10	12.006	13.181	14.487	15.938	17.549	19.337	25.959
11	13.486	14.972	16.646	18.531	20.655	23.045	32.150
12	15.026	16.870	18.977	21.385	24.133	27.271	39.580
13	16.627	18.882	21.495	24.523	28.029	32.089	48.497
14	18.292	21.015	24.215	27.976	32.393	37.581	59.196
15	20.024	23.276	27.152	31.773	37.280	43.842	72.035
16	21.825	25.673	30.324	35.950	42.753	50.980	87.442
17	23.698	28.213	33.750	40.546	48.884	59.118	105.930
18	25.645	30.906	37.450	45.600	55.750	68.394	128.120
19	27.671	33.760	41.446	51.160	63.440	78.969	154.740
20	29.778	36.778	45.762	57.276	75.052	91.025	186.690
30	56.085	79.058	113.283	164.496	241.330	356.790	1181.900
40	95.026	154.762	259.057	442.597	767.090	1342.000	7343.900

TABLE 3: PRESENT VALUE OF $1 = PVIF = T3

Periods	4%	6%	8%	10%	12%	14%	20%
1	0.962	0.943	0.926	0.909	0.893	0.877	0.833
2	0.925	0.890	0.857	0.826	0.797	0.769	0.694
3	0.889	0.840	0.794	0.751	0.712	0.675	0.579
4	0.855	0.792	0.735	0.683	0.636	0.592	0.482
5	0.822	0.747	0.681	0.621	0.567	0.519	0.402
6	0.790	0.705	0.630	0.564	0.507	0.456	0.335
7	0.760	0.665	0.583	0.513	0.452	0.400	0.279
8	0.731	0.627	0.540	0.467	0.404	0.351	0.233
9	0.703	0.592	0.500	0.424	0.361	0.308	0.194
10	0.676	0.558	0.463	0.386	0.322	0.270	0.162
11	0.650	0.527	0.429	0.350	0.287	0.237	0.135
12	0.625	0.497	0.397	0.319	0.257	0.208	0.112
13	0.601	0.469	0.368	0.290	0.229	0.182	0.093
14	0.577	0.442	0.340	0.263	0.205	0.160	0.078
15	0.555	0.417	0.315	0.239	0.183	0.140	0.065
16	0.534	0.394	0.292	0.218	0.163	0.123	0.054
17	0.513	0.371	0.270	0.198	0.146	0.108	0.045
18	0.494	0.350	0.250	0.180	0.130	0.095	0.038
19	0.475	0.331	0.232	0.164	0.116	0.083	0.031
20	0.456	0.312	0.215	0.149	0.104	0.073	0.026
30	0.308	0.174	0.099	0.057	0.033	0.020	0.004
40	0.208	0.097	0.046	0.022	0.011	0.005	0.001

TABLE 4: PRESENT VALUE OF AN ANNUITY OF $1 =
PVIFA =T4

Periods	4%	6%	8%	10%	12%	14%	20%
1	0.962	0.943	0.926	0.909	0.893	0.877	0.833
2	1.886	1.833	1.783	1.736	1.690	1.647	1.528
3	2.775	2.673	2.577	2.487	2.402	2.322	2.106
4	3.630	3.465	3.312	3.170	3.037	2.914	2.589
5	4.452	4.212	3.993	3.791	3.605	3.433	2.991
6	5.242	4.917	4.623	4.355	4.111	3.889	3.326
7	6.002	5.582	5.206	4.868	4.564	4.288	3.605
8	6.733	6.210	5.747	5.335	4.968	4.639	3.837
9	7.435	6.802	6.247	5.759	5.328	4.946	4.031
10	8.111	7.360	6.710	6.145	5.650	5.216	4.192
11	8.760	7.887	7.139	6.495	5.938	5.453	4.327
12	9.385	8.384	7.536	6.814	6.194	5.660	4.439
13	9.986	8.853	7.904	7.103	6.424	5.842	4.533
14	10.563	9.295	8.244	7.367	6.628	6.002	4.611
15	11.118	9.712	8.559	7.606	6.811	6.142	4.675
16	11.652	10.106	8.851	7.824	6.974	6.265	4.730
17	12.168	10.477	9.122	8.022	7.120	6.373	4.775
18	12.659	10.828	9.372	8.201	7.250	6.467	4.812
19	13.134	11.158	9.604	8.365	7.366	6.550	4.844
20	13.590	11.470	9.818	8.514	7.469	6.623	4.870
30	17.292	13.765	11.258	9.427	8.055	7.003	4.979
40	19.793	15.046	11.925	9.779	8.244	7.105	4.997